DATE DUE

WAY OFF THE ROAD

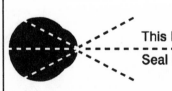

This Large Print Book carries the
Seal of Approval of N.A.V.H.

WAY OFF THE ROAD

DISCOVERING THE PECULIAR CHARMS OF SMALL-TOWN AMERICA

BILL GEIST

THORNDIKE PRESS

An imprint of Thomson Gale, a part of The Thomson Corporation

THOMSON

*

™

GALE

Detroit • New York • San Francisco • New Haven, Conn. • Waterville, Maine • London

THOMSON

GALE

LIBRARY OF CONGRESS CATALOGING-IN-PUBLICATION DATA

Geist, William.
    Way off the road : discovering the peculiar charms of small-town America / by Bill Geist.
        p. cm. — (Thorndike Press large print laugh lines)
    ISBN-13: 978-0-7862-9643-9 (hardcover : alk. paper)
    ISBN-10: 0-7862-9643-7 (hardcover : alk. paper)
    1. United States — Social life and customs — 1971 — Anecdotes. 2. United States — Social life and customs — 1971 — Humor. 3. City and town life — United States — Anecdotes. 4. City and town life — United States — Humor. 5. United States — Biography — Anecdotes. 6. United States — History, Local — Anecdotes. 7. Cities and towns — United States — Anecdotes. 8. Geist, William — Travel — United States — Anecdotes. 9. American wit and humor. 10. Large type books. I. Title.
    E169.Z83G45 2007b
    973.923—dc22

                                                        2007010232

Published in 2007 by arrangement with Broadway Books,
a division of Random House, Inc.

Printed in the United States of America on permanent paper
10 9 8 7 6 5 4 3 2 1

For Jody, Libby, Christina, Willie,
and little TBD

DISCOVERING THE PECULAR CHARMS OF SMALL-TOWN AMERICA

CONTENTS

AUTHOR'S NOTE

This book is 100 percent celebrity free. It contains no trace elements of "red" or "blue" states or other corrosive political toxins. Contents are all-natural, free-range, organic nonfiction with no synthetic additives to enhance size or performance. People with wood pulp allergies should not eat this book. Same goes for beavers. Taken optically as directed it has zero carbohydrates and zero grams of trans fat. No animals were harmed, no press credentials required, and no public relations representatives involved in the manufacture of this book. If you experience an erection lasting for more than four hours while using this product, I'd be really surprised. Pregnant women should not operate heavy machinery during childbirth. Contains no miracle diet, no key to riches, no names or e-mail addresses of the people you'll meet in heaven. No refunds. No batteries required. May cause restless leg syndrome or inoperable brain tumors. We don't know. We still don't really know much of anything for sure, now do we?

INTRODUCTION

There is a world outside our own, out there and out of sight, between the coasts — between Philadelphia and Pittsburgh, Chicago and St. Louis, Kansas City and Denver — where people live slower, closer to nature, farther apart spatially, yet somehow more attached; a world where money, celebrity, and raw ambition don't always hold sway, and where people tend not to take themselves quite so seriously. This book is about that vanishing rural world from whence we all came at one time and place or another.

It is also about celebrating unique individuals who are resourceful, eccentric, idiosyncratic, and at times just plain batty — yet oddly inspiring: an entrepreneur who ingeniously sucks problematic prairie dogs out of the ground with a sewer vacuum; a ninety-two-year-old publisher-pilot who delivers his newspapers by plane; the sole resident of a town who, as mayor, must hold public hearings with herself.

The year 2007 marks twenty years that I've been on the road for CBS, and I've seen a lot of unusual things. This thought occurs to me while watching a thousand sword-wielding medieval soldiers in full battle regalia and battle cry come charging down the side of a piney ravine toward a rendezvous with an opposing army stampeding down the other side. The warriors slash, stab, and spear one another with rattan weapons all the way up to the lunch break. Boy, if the people just over the hill on I-59 could see this! I am the only audience to this epic battle, which takes place outside Lumberton, Mississippi (pop: 2,228), in the twenty-first century, but no one here seems to realize this, lost as they are in their weekend medieval personas, eating medieval fare, wearing authentic garb, and speaking in stilted medieval language. For the likes of King Alarek of the Kingdom of Ans Theora (Texas and Oklahoma) and Orm the Wanderer of Trimaris (Florida), indeed for all the viscounts, dukes, exchequers, and others, it's going to be tough to snap out of it back at the office on Monday morning. They refer to this as returning to the "Mundane World." Indeed.

There is nothing of the Mundane World here. The people in this book live in the Mundane World but are not of it.

Traveling to forty-nine states, I have learned much about this nation, but few overarching truths except to say that, truth is, there aren't many that hold true. I've learned that the Amish play a mean game of donkey basketball (a Midwestern thing, where basketball players ride donkeys). Who knew? I thought they were like Quaker pacifists, but the night I saw them play in Middlefield, Ohio (pop: 2,233) they were ferociously competitive and aggressive in overpowering the firemen's team. Fans packed the gym and filled the parking lot with their buggies. America is full of surprises.

We don't learn much about our country on the interstates, except that Americans are in a hell of a hurry and happily trade speed for wonder and discovery. Today Tocqueville would cross the country on I-80 from Jersey to Frisco, faithfully recording the exit numbers; Kerouac's *On the Road* would take place in an endlessly repeating pattern of

Holiday Inns and Denny's; Least Heat-Moon would author *Green Interstate Highways*.

Flying, of course, is even worse. On a trip from Los Angeles to New York, crossing the Rockies on a clear day, I gaze down in awe, contemplating these majestic peaks when a flight attendant comes on the PA and orders us to pull down our window shades so that we can better enjoy today's in-flight movie, *Dude, Where's My Car?*

I don't mind saying that in twenty years I have gained a measure of fame. One Sunday morning outside Lebanon, Indiana (pop: 14,222), I rang a farmhouse doorbell to ask if our crew could get a shot of the basketball hoop on their barn. I could see through the sheer curtain on the door window that the family was watching television. A young boy of about ten opened the door and took a step backward, wide-eyed and in an apparent state of shock. "It's him!" he shouted. "It's the guy on TV!" I looked past him and saw that a segment of mine was at that moment showing on their screen. After explaining about the hoop, I told the family that we like to get out and personally thank each viewer for watching the show.

I didn't know when I started that this book was going to be about small towns. I began writing about my favorite experiences and, after I'd written eight, realized they'd all occurred in very small towns. Why, I'm not really sure.

A return to my roots? My parents ran a country newspaper, the *Fisher Reporter,* in Fisher, Illinois (pop: 1,647), with some coverage of news from other towns in the Greater Fisher Metro Area, towns with quirky names like Normal and Oblong. My father's favorite headline was OBLONG WOMAN MARRIES NORMAL MAN.

They moved to the big city, Champaign (pop: 60,000, then), where I grew up. It was still pretty provincial. I realized in flipping through an old yearbook recently that our foreign exchange student was from America. Hawaii. Who knew?

I made my way to Chicago, which my father had warned me was full of all manner of evil and badness: crime, filth, immorality, Democrats . . . It was a new world of subway trains and skyscrapers and somehow tolerated intolerables: unending traffic jams, cramped quarters, and everyday rudeness that would get you punched out back where I came from. The suburbs tried to pretend they were small towns, except there were two hundred of them cemented together, literally, and attached to the city.

If Chicago was to me a different world, New York was an entirely different planet, light-years from Normal. People lived in NASA nose-cone-size apartments, in threatening neighborhoods near nothing, with smelly trash on the sidewalks (somebody *forgot the alleys* when New York was built), and paid exorbitant prices for the privilege. There were people in Manhattan, which is legally part of America, who didn't own TV sets or cars!

You could read fellow passengers' watches and newspapers on the subway. Restaurant tables were so small and close together (two inches) you practically had to eat without using your arms, like it was a pie-eating or apple-bobbing contest. Fellow human beings came to be considered obstacles: in restaurants, on the roads, on the sidewalks. A cabdriver disclosed to me: "I've always considered courtesy a sign of weakness."

It was all endlessly fascinating, in a Jane Goodall sort of way, and I loved the excitement of walking in New York, where energy seemed to be shooting from the sidewalks right up into my shoes. But subconsciously I needed relief from this Tasered rat race once in a while, needed to get back to where I came from, back in place and time.

People ask me: But aren't small towns boring? You betcha! And boredom has consequences, as you're about to see. Michael Carmichael, of Alexandria, Indiana (pop: 5,868), uses his extra time to continue expanding his world's largest paintball, a baseball he's painted over the past thirty years with 18,049 coats of paint at the time we visited (more than 20,000 coats by now), weighing about 1,300 pounds with a circumference of more than nine feet. Out in South Dakota, sculptor Korczak Ziolkowski decided in 1947 to carve a likeness of Chief Crazy Horse, one that dwarfs Mount Rushmore and is larger than the Sphinx, from a mountain out behind the house. His family continues the dynamite-sculpting and it should be finished in just a few more generations.

Let others report "Britney's Breakup"; let them spread today's truth from White House officials and countermand it tomorrow; and let them report "Are Terrorists Targeting Our Applebee's?"

My beat is finding seemingly ordinary people doing extraordinary things: a photographer who specializes exclusively in portraits of cows; a chef whose specialty is roadkill; a town too small for a traditional parade solves the problem by having the watchers walk around the standstill "marchers."

These people, places, and events are news to me.

STANDSTILL PARADE

WHALAN, MINNESOTA, POP: 62

Whalan, Minnesota, is a bucolic little town. But you know what? Things can get a little *too* bucolic sometimes. The unlocked front doors, the peace and quiet, and the down-home neighborliness are all well and good, but from time to time folks want a little excitement for a change.

"Let's have a parade!" proposed the young, vivacious, ponytailed local business-man and fairly new guy in town David Har-renstein. Hmmm. Nice idea, but next to impossible in a town where the population is sixty-two and dropping fast, numerically and quite literally.

Whalan has none of your essential parade elements, according to town council member Buddy Olson. A marching band? "No." Fire truck? "No." Police car? "No." A queen of any kind? "No." Buddy isn't going negative on us, just stating the facts. All of this is not to mention the biggest problem of all, parade-wise: the whole town's only, at the most, two blocks long. A parade would be over before it began.

"Everybody loves a parade," David says. "We're just geographically challenged." He admits to an ulterior motive. David owns the Overland Inn, one of the only buildings in town. It's no longer an inn, but a small restaurant of sorts that serves ice cream and "world-famous pie" — world famous around here at least. He wanted to attract some people to town, people who like pie à la mode. Since purchasing the inn two years earlier, he'd found doing business without people around to be extremely challenging.

Townsfolk were skeptical, as small-town folk often are when it comes to new ideas. "We've never had a parade," says Harley Olson, Buddy's father. "At least not since '43, when I got here. About, oooh, forty years ago we did have a carnival, but it's been pretty quiet since." Adeline Larson backed him up on that, saying she could not recollect a parade in her eighty-eight years here.

Then David came up with a breakthrough idea — maybe even a concept. To solve the paramount problem of a parade being too long for their short town, why not have the parade stand still — stay with him on this — and have the crowd walk around it? A stand-still parade!

"We were gonna lock him up when he said that," Buddy scoffs. But the more Buddy and others in town got to thinking about it, the more they thought: You know, it just might work.

Not to bring up a sore subject, but what would be *in* the parade?

You need a cop car with a siren and flashing lights, for openers. The Fillmore County sheriff had one and said he supposed he could send it over, since there really ought to be a police presence at a major public event like this.

You need a color guard. Old-timer Marvin Severson, commander of the local American Legion post, had to be convinced to deploy his forces. He said he was a little out of practice: "The last parade I was in was up in Black River Falls in '52." But Marvin came around. The flag-bearing Legionnaires would lead the parade, right behind the police car. They're old, but they could still stand, which was all that would be required.

David named Adeline, the town's oldest living resident, as grand marshal. She, too, resisted the honor. "I finally agreed after he told me I wouldn't have to do anything," she says. "I guess in this parade nobody does anything."

You need smiling, waving politicians in a parade, but that's never a problem. State Representative Greg Davids said sure, he'd be there. "I march in one or two parades every Saturday, and when I heard there was no walking involved in this one, I said, 'Now *this* is a good parade.' "

As mentioned, Whalan has no queen; nary a corn queen or a soybean queen or any other royalty for that matter. So David invited the Lanesboro Beef Queen, whom he described as "quite slender, actually."

Nearby Lanesboro, a major city in these parts (pop: 775), turned out to be a friendly neighbor in need, agreeing to send a fire truck, an ambulance, and the high school's marching band, which could possibly be deprogrammed to not march.

Now we're talking!

Word spread of this revolutionary new parade concept and David was besieged by entries: Boy Scouts, polka bands, dog groomers, you name it. The parade was becoming almost too big even to stand still within the Whalan city limits.

Locals began sprucing up the town, giving a small building on the main street a fresh coat of paint, mowing lawns, and sweeping sidewalks. Women began making lefse, a kind of a potato-dough tortilla, a Norwegian delicacy, not recommended by doctors, to sell at the parade. There are many Nordics in Minnesota. Many, many, many.

Parade day dawns a perfect, warm, sunny Saturday in May. Downtown Whalan is bustling with more people probably than had ever been here before — certainly at one time, and perhaps cumulatively (founded: 1876).

David needs a walkie-talkie to coordinate the event. This being the worldwide premiere of the Concept, without a rehearsal, there are many questions: a fellow decked out in 1890s garb shows up riding one of those antique tall-wheeled unicycles. How is he supposed to ride it in the parade if he has to remain motionless?

"Does it have a kickstand?" David asks helpfully.

A theatrical troupe asks for an official ruling on this question: With this being a standstill parade, were they allowed to do song-and-dance numbers? David decrees they can, so long as they stay within their designated space.

A barricade is set up in front of the parade. Then comes the sheriff's car, followed by an impressive ten-Legionnaire color guard. Way to go Marvin! After that it was first come, first served in the parade lineup.

Now, how does a standstill parade start? "I don't know," David replies. "We're breaking new ground. I think it just sort of happens."

And, sure enough, it does. The police car's siren wails. The well-disciplined color guard stands still. The car carrying Grand Marshal Adeline Larson remains in "Park," and she begins to wave, albeit to the same three people. And the fifteen-piece marching band becomes a band stand, striking up "It's a Grand Old Flag."

There are floats, not so much of the Rose Bowl Parade variety, but more in the tacksome-tinsel-to-the-edge-of-a-flatbed-truck style. There's a bluegrass band, a white poodle in a hat and sunglasses having her nails painted in the back of a dog groomer's truck, and seven Boy Scouts from — where else? — Lanesboro.

Two (not all that entertaining) people in the parade are just sitting on bales of hay, and complaining a little about their placement "over here by the septic system." And in a standstill parade, that is not about to change.

28

As usual, horses bring up the rear. "I guess they put us back here out of habit," says one rider. "But it's not necessary in this parade. No one's going to step in anything." The nature of the parade allows one participant, a professional masseuse, to set up her table and offer complimentary services.

Members of the unprecedented crowd have come from as far away as Wyzeta (150 miles) and now stand almost one deep all along the parade route. "We haven't had this many people in Whalan since the bank closed in '32," says one member of a polka band "riding" in a classic old red convertible and promoting Das Wurst Haus in Lanesboro. Lanesboro really has it all.

But the crowd doesn't quite *get* it. They're standing still or sitting in lawn chairs, the way you would at a normal parade. When the band plays "Anchors Aweigh" the crowd remains anchored to the curb.

Finally, after some prompting and explanation, they slowly begin to stroll around the parade. ("Norwegians are slow learners," quips a Swede.) A few stop to pet the horses or to chat with members of the parade, things you simply could not do within the old parade paradigm. Others actually meander among the parade units, going where no parade-goers have gone before.

They're eating David's pie and ice cream. The lefse is selling like hotcakes, which they sort of are, as are copies of the best-selling book (here) *91 Ways to Serve Lefse.*

A woman from Wyzeta takes it all in and says, "This is America"; to which George Judy, a local resident wearing a plaid shirt and denim overalls, replies, "It is now. Everybody's getting goofy."

He's right about that, of course, and here everyone seems to be enjoying getting goofy and they're giving the parade rave reviews. "It's ecologically sound," says one viewer, "and it's easier to take pictures." A man named Ernie, driving a stunning '32 Packard — one of several antique cars in the lineup — notes that this is the first parade where he doesn't have to worry about running out of gas or having an overheated engine.

Even before it's over, David pronounces that there will definitely be a Second Annual Whalan Parade, and that it will be even better next year. "We need a reviewing stand. Maybe we could put it on a flatbed truck and drive it around the parade. Maybe put some of the audience on bleachers on a flatbed too." The man is a parade savant! He figures he'd better put a cap on the number of parade entries next year, too, or enlarge the town. And, order more Porta-Johns.

So, how do you know when a standstill parade is over? "I don't know," David admits. Apparently it's when things start moving. The horses are bored by all this standing around and break ranks. The sheriff's car pulls away, the color guard rolls up their American Legion banner, the masseuse folds up her table, the band marches, and everybody goes home. Happy. It's been an exciting day in Whalan, perhaps the first.

THE FLYING PAPERBOY

LOYALTON, CALIFORNIA, POP: 817

A small plane, a red speck on the vast, blue western sky, flies lazily high above a rancher's house. Then suddenly it dips its left wing, makes a sharp turn, and dives nearly to the desert floor before leveling off and making a run straight at the house, rather menacingly, like a fighter plane on the attack.

Clearly, the pilot is on a mission, the house his target. And, indeed, as the plane buzzes over, it drops . . . something . . . small . . . that lands not fifty feet from the porch, a bull's-eye. "You want it close, but not *on* the house," the pilot and bombardier explains, looking back out his window to see someone scurry to pick it up and wave.

Another successful operation for veteran flying ace Hal Wright, who publishes the *Sierra Booster* newspaper in Loyalton, California, and delivers it by air drop — with smart-bomb accuracy — to subscribers living on far-flung ranches.

It's hard to believe that with some thirty-six million people now jammed into California, there can still be places as completely out of the way as the old mining town of Loyalton. It accounts for just a few hundred of those thirty-six million residents, and lies in a peaceful valley of the Sierra Nevada mountain range northwest of Reno, Nevada. It's surrounded by ranches that sprouted up back during the gold rush of the 1850s to provide dairy products and beef for the mine workers.

We found but one place that puts people up for the night, the Golden West Saloon, where you walk in and expect to see Miss Kitty and Marshal Dillon having a drink at the bar. The few rooms are on the second floor and their doors open out onto a walkway overlooking the bar, just like at the Longbranch on *Gunsmoke*. Pay phone's down the hall.

Next morning, we meet Hal, a fit and frisky ninety-two-year-old, who tells us he was once a local gold digger himself, until he fell down a mine shaft, and lived to pledge he'd never go back. He and his wife, who's named Allene, but whom he refers to only as "Sweetie Pie," somehow got what he calls "this harebrained idea" to start a newspaper. The first edition of the *Sierra Booster* is dated October 21, 1949, and includes a front-page note to readers: "To be published fortnightly at Loyalton, California, until further notice." Hal never gave any such notice and has no plans to.

As publisher, he hired himself as editor, who hired himself as the reporter, columnist, and photographer, as well as the production and advertising staffs. I accompany Hal on his rounds, as he stops at a few of the few area businesses to sell advertising — and ask for news: maybe they'd heard something interesting. "We have a new plumbing room," offers the woman behind the counter at the hardware store, and Hal makes note of it. "You can't print anywhere near all the news that's going on," Hal explains to me, walking at his usual fast pace out of the store. "You just can't do it."

There are no headlines in his newspaper; Hal doesn't like to sensationalize. There are photographs of local cats and dogs, a popular feature, and columns bearing news from surrounding towns, such as "The Downieville Dragnet."

A big story in the current edition informs readers that the "animal control officer" no longer wants to be called the "dogcatcher," and perhaps never did. "We thought that was newsworthy," Hal explains, adding that the position of the newspaper on this issue is that "dogcatcher" is just fine.

Hal's column, which he gives prominent placement, attacks the Federal Aviation Administration for trying to "clip his wings," that is, for trying to deny him a renewal of his pilot's license. Ultimately, Hal won.

"That was strictly age discrimination," Hal says. "I had to hire three doctors and one attorney in order to get the job done."

Hal is the oldest licensed pilot in the nation. He joined the UFOs (United Flying Octogenarians) — although technically he's too old. Has he considered starting a club for nonagenarian pilots? "No," he answers, "I don't want to be the president, secretary, treasurer, and the board of directors."

In addition to his other duties at the *Sierra Booster,* Hal is also in charge of circulation and is its only paperboy. In this sparsely populated area, with subscribers scattered over six hundred square miles, he decided to deliver papers to the ranches in his airplane.

Hal invites me along on his paper route.

Driving out to the airstrip, he tells of his three (or is it five?) heart operations, at which point our cameraman, Gilbert, says that, although he'd love to come along, he'll be mounting a camera inside the cockpit and staying on the ground. It's a sunny day. I mention to Hal that his windshield wipers are on.

Hal has a small plane: a four-seater Aeronca, which was brand new in 1949. I strap myself in while Hal loads newspapers and starts the engine . . . no, wait, it's not starting. Won't start. A tow truck arrives twenty minutes later to jump-start the engine — although at this point I'm kind of hoping it won't. I ask if the tow truck provides aerial service should that become necessary.

As the plane finally revs its little old (single) engine and begins to roll — rather slowly, it seems to me — down the runway, I imagine a stewardess coming on the intercom: "Good morning. Your captain on this morning's flight is three-time heart surgery survivor Hal Wright, the oldest living pilot, who hired a lawyer to successfully overturn the FAA's rejection of his license renewal on a legal technicality. Now sit back, relax, and enjoy the flight."

Just before liftoff, Hal Wright mentions

that he is a cousin of Orville and Wilbur. An older cousin? "No, they were a bit older," he says.

At about a thousand feet or so, Hal levels her off and reaches into the pile of newspapers in the backseat. Holding the yoke (or as I call it the "steering wheel") between his knees, Hal begins to hum a tune while folding a paper into a tightly tucked square.

"Not to be a backseat driver," I say, "but there's a mountain right in front of us."

"Ohhh yeahhh, thanks, I hadn't noticed that," Hal replies, making a slow left turn. I pray he's joking. "I wonder who put that there?" he adds. "It wasn't there yesterday."

Then he suddenly makes a sharp turn and dives, down to about 150 feet (or was it 15?), where he levels off and heads toward a ranch. He slides back his window, grabs a paper, and without benefit of bombardier instruments, deftly lets it fly at precisely the right moment.

Hal makes a second pass and sees the rancher, Chuck Howes, waving and picking up the paper not fifty feet from his front door — a lot closer than I get mine delivered at home. "Sometimes it's closer, and sometimes it's farther away," Howes tells me later, "but Hal drops them right in the yard. He dropped one in the pigpen one time down there. I didn't go for that one." Hal has but one mishap this day, at another ranch, where the paper comes untucked and floats down in sections: presumably news, sports, arts and leisure.

For some of his more remote subscribers, the newspaper dropping out of the sky is a much anticipated happening. Hal might consider also dropping mail and groceries. At one ranch, a woman and her two small children are outside and waving when Hal flies over. Out here they can hear his plane coming a mile away. When the paper hits the ground the children race to pick it up.

But outsiders witnessing an airdrop for the first time don't quite know what to make of it, according to Hal's daughter, Jan. "He was throwing the paper out over Route 395, and the highway patrol saw him and called it in. They met him at the airport and they thought for sure it was a drug drop." Today, Homeland Security would scramble the F-15s.

The videotape of our flight will later reveal my face turning a bit green and my overall demeanor becoming somewhat less cheerful as the dive-bombing delivery mission continues. Recalling the jump-start, the FAA's rejection letter, and the open-heart surgeries, I ask Hal, in a calm voice meant to show interest rather than concern, "So Hal, if you wanted to land this thing, do you push forward on this steering wheel thing to make it slow down?"

Hal smiles, resumes humming, and — again holding the steering wheel thing between his knees — picks up his camera and starts snapping a few aerial shots for the next edition of the *Booster,* which has been coming out for nearly half a century with no "further notice" on the horizon.

Prairie Dog Suckers

Colorado is best known for its Rocky Mountains, but many attractions lie in the southwestern part, where the Rockies aren't.

Outside Monte Vista, on Route 160, sits the Movie Manor Motel, where guests like myself can lie in bed indoors and watch an outdoor drive-in movie with the sound piped in. Everybody thought George Kelloff was nuts when he built a motel facing his drive-in movie screen, but that was forty years ago and it's still flourishing.

Close by is the famous Four Corners, where four states come together at one point and Indians sell trinkets and snacks from makeshift plywood booths to tourists who drive from thousands of miles away to see the spot. Frankly, I was dumbfounded by it, perplexed and not really knowing what to think or say about this point where Colorado, Arizona, New Mexico, and Utah come together. After putting my arms and legs in four different states, I hit the road.

And there is the breathtaking, awe-inspiring Mesa Verde National Park, where ancient Pueblo Indians carved whole towns into the sides of cliffs.

But we're not going to talk about any of that right now. We're going to talk about Gay Balfour, of nearby Cortez, Colorado, inventor of a miraculous machine that's changing the face of the western landscape and pet stores everywhere. It's an inspiring tale of faith and spirituality, of a fantastic dream realized, and of good old-fashioned American ingenuity.

Colorado may be a home where the majestic buffalo once roamed, but what you mostly see these days are swarms of furry little rodents scurrying around, chewing up the alfalfa fields and digging holes that fracture farm machinery and the legs of horses and cattle: prairie dogs, barking squirrels, sod poodles, scourge of man, and last on the list of zoo-goers everywhere.

Farmers in these parts like Walter Tell had tried everything to get rid of the burrowing varmints — including Weapons of Mass Destruction! "We've tried gas, poison, shooting them, everything," told Tell. Other farmers and ranchers tried drowning and flamethrowers. Havahart traps were never considered.

Balfour, a welder and machine-shop owner by trade, was down on his luck, trying to make his fortune with a marina on a nearby reservoir. But he couldn't keep it afloat, financially speaking, bedeviled as he was by governmental agencies and the bank — two of your top bedevilers. The bank finally stepped in and took the marina, his machine shop, and pretty much everything he had.

His wife, Judy, suggested he ask the Lord for help, which he did. He prayed about loans and regulations, but it didn't seem to be working. Judy suggested he make his prayers less specific (maybe God doesn't like paperwork), which he did. And then Gay Balfour had a dream: not that one day all mankind would live together in peace and harmony, but rather that a big yellow truck could suck prairie dogs out of the ground with long green hoses. He didn't think right away that this was the answer to his prayers, just a really weird dream.

The next day, he had a welding job on the Ute Mountain Indian reservation, repairing a farm irrigation system. But the farmers there were more concerned about a bigger problem. Their land was being overrun by swarms of prairie dogs, which were digging up the seed corn and making cavernous holes that broke the harvesting equipment. The tribe had been pouring poison down the holes to no avail. It was like the critters were sitting down there kicking back in little hazmat suits.

Balfour told the Indians he just might have an idea, although he didn't dare tell them he'd dreamed of a prairie dog vacuum for fear they'd think he'd been hitting the peace pipe.

Hoover doesn't make anything quite big enough for a job like this, so he stopped by the local sanitation department to see if maybe he could borrow the sewer vacuum truck. And he swears that before he could get the words out, the superintendent asked him if he'd like to buy their old vacuum truck. He did. It was yellow. His next stop was at an industrial supply store where he found big hoses. Green hoses. Yes, the Lord works in mysterious ways.

The vacuum is called a Vac-All, and Gay Balfour was about to put that name to the test. He rigged up the truck and returned to the Indian reservation, where he proceeded to suck up twenty-three dazed prairie dogs in forty-five minutes. The Ute Indians immediately signed him to a $6,000 contract. Sure, you could say if it'd been the *Cleveland* Indians the figure would have been more like $6 million, but Gay was happy, and after he'd sucked 750 prairie dogs out of these sacred grounds, the Indians were gay too. Happy gay.

A business was born, offering the latest in rodent control technology; environmentally friendly, utilizing no deadly poisons, and people friendly, what with fewer stray bullets intended for prairie dogs flying around. I mean, some of these problem dogs were in residential neighborhoods. Gay named his new business Dog Gone, and felt confident enough to buy yellow Dog Gone baseball caps and T-shirts for himself and his employee, Dave Honaker, a relative.

Word of the dog suckers began to spread far and wide as the two barnstormed to vanquish this peril of the plains. They were called in by tormented towns in several states throughout the west as hired guns to take out the evil intruders and return life to normal. Now, when I say "take out," I mean some of the prairie dogs were relocated, while others were "taken out" more in the mafioso or military sense, that is, relocated to whatever sort of afterlife prairie dogs believe in. Gay sold them as food to federal breeding programs for endangered species, such as black-footed ferrets, and to rehab programs for injured hawks, eagles, and owls.

The two men successfully removed prairie dogs — sometimes at the rate of more than 150 per day — from soccer fields in Durango, a Christian Living Campus in Denver, farms and housing developments in Kansas, Nebraska, and Alberta, Canada. They sucked 'em up at racetracks, airports, even at a high-security Air Force base, where the prairie dogs were setting off motion detectors. Clients were being charged on a per-dog basis or a set fee of thousands of dollars a day. (The firm now employs Gay's wife, their two daughters, ten of his thirteen grandchildren, and the occasional cousin.)

When they go to work they say they're "goin' doggin' " and it's something to see. Under a big blue sky, with the mountains as a backdrop, Gay and Dave slowly prowl the plains in their yellow truck, marked with the company logo (a prairie dog being swept up in a tornado) and Dog Gone inscribed on the side. They don't go in for camouflage or subterfuge; plus, prairie dogs are functionally illiterate.

Gay drives while Dave scans the open fields with binoculars. The chirping prairie dogs sit up on their tails, crane their necks, and look back. When the men spot a dog ducking down a hole, they stop the truck, start the loud motor on the Vac-All and insert the hose into the top few inches of the hole.

Dave mans the tube, which shudders a mite in his hands as pebbles and dirt fly through. Often nothing more happens. Some of these tunnel complexes feature several exits, as well as nesting rooms, listening rooms, family rooms — veritable underground McMansions that would make the Vietcong proud.

"It's like drilling for oil," Gay says. "Sometimes you come up dry." He noted that this was the heat of the day, when dogs keep cool underground and don't show their positions. Your dogs-per-hour (DPH) rate drops.

On their third hole, they strike dog. Dave can feel it. The tube draws still and there is a rising whine to the engine. He feels the resistance as the critter tries to maintain a foothold. He even has a feel for the size of the dog. When Dave gives a thumbs-up all eyes are on the twenty-seven-foot translucent tube, waiting to see a dark lump cruising through at about forty-five miles per hour into the back of the truck, where it hits a foam-rubber wall.

Some animal rights activists don't particularly approve of Dog Gone, to the point of organizing a call-in and write-in protest in one town where Gay did business. Frankly, the process looked to me like something humans pay good money to do to themselves at Six Flags: a thrill ride. Did Gay ever consider getting a bigger tube and selling tickets to humans? "Nope," he says, "but we thought about a big tube for riot control. It would work, too, if you got a bigger unit."

He also has the idea of maybe trying to sell these demi-dogs as a delicacy to the French, who seem to eat pretty much anything so long as it's concealed under a nice sauce.

The prairie dogs I saw crawling around in the back of the truck seemed unscathed — dazed and confused to be sure, but physically unharmed. (I'm not qualified to speak to the issue of post-traumatic prairie dog stress syndrome.) In fact, for many of these prairie dogs, it may be the best thing that can happen; gets 'em out of the food chain for a while so they can relax.

The prairie dogs are transferred, very carefully, with big heavy-duty gloves to protect against their teeth and claws, from inside the truck's chamber to a wire cage on the outside. Dave feeds them some alfalfa and softly talks to them to calm them down. Not in English. He's taken the time and effort to learn their native tongue, and is able to communicate with them in their own chirp-and-bark dialect. And they speak back. Dave won't say what they talk about.

"They're a little surprised," Dave says, reflecting on the prairie dogs' current state of mind. "They weren't expecting anything like this."

And if they're surprised now, just wait until they see where they're going.

Gay and Dave did a job in Amarillo, Texas, where they sucked only young prairie dogs (six to ten weeks old) by dialing down the power. (That's how sophisticated this industry, still in its infancy, has already become!) They sold them to a middleman for $25 per dog, who in turn wholesaled them to pet stores. Yes, prairie dogs (these of the Gunnison's breed) are becoming trendy exotic pets. Especially good for small apartments, they fetch $450 apiece in New York. Others are being exported to Japan, where they sell for $700 in Tokyo shops. Global markets!

In this area of nearly tapped-out gold, silver, and platinum mines, Gay Balfour and Dave Honaker are tapping into another underground mother lode, turning menacing pests into a cash crop, and helping restore America's balance of trade.

"Doesn't that just beat all?" laughs rancher Walter Tell, a satisfied Dog Gone customer. "A prairie dog for a pet? It'd never happen around here" — like having a pet cockroach in New York.

THE CHURCH OF THE HOLY BBQ

HUNTSVILLE, TEXAS, POP: 35,840

Smoke billows from the small clapboard building on Montgomery Road, nearly engulfing the place and obscuring the church next door.

It looks to be a four-alarm in progress, and there's not a firefighter in sight. But someone's entering the building . . . and someone else is coming out . . . slowly, calmly . . . carrying a bag . . .

A bag of barbecue, the best around. Some say the best in all of Texas, or at least the world. And that's a mouthful, what with some 1,300 barbecue joints in the state, most of them here in the Barbecue Belt that stretches from the central hill country to the Louisiana border. In Texas barbecue is a religion, though not yet taught in theological seminaries, and nowhere more so than here in Huntsville at this little BBQ joint known in these parts as "The Church of the Holy Barbecue."

Local firefighters have actually been summoned here by concerned passersby who didn't realize that the restaurant was not afire, it just looked that way. The smoke belches from two big ol' soot-blackened barbecue pits, tended by one big ol' soot-covered man, who really ought to be wearing an OSHA-mandated, oxygen-equipped gas mask if ever one was needed for any job, anywhere. Instead he sits there in his baseball cap and bib overalls on a folding chair that he's pulled up real close so he can work the damper, feed the wood fire, and tend the meats. Holding his job looks to be the rough equivalent of a ten-packs-a-day habit.

Says his name is Howard, that he's been sitting there daily for about twenty years and doesn't really mind the smoke. And, after all, he basks in a perpetual baptism of what many around here call "the holy smoke," a divine ambrosial incense that flavors the heavenly ribs, brisket, chicken, links, and Howard, although he says no one has ever tried to sneak up on him with a knife and fork.

"People think our secret's the wood," he says. "They want to buy our wood, but I tell 'em it's just plain old wood, whatever they bring us. That ain't it." So . . . what *is* . . . it?

Howard sits before the formerly white but now nicely browned restaurant that is "The Church of the Holy Barbecue." It's actual, God-given name is the New Zion Missionary Baptist Church Barbecue, just a gnawed rib-bone's toss away from the little red-brick church itself.

Annie Mae Ward, then, would be the pope of the church barbecue, which she founded and operates with the aid of a few other church sisters. They arrive early, doing the Lord's work under the watchful eyes of Jesus, whose face is that of the kitchen clock. The church ladies can be seen in the open kitchen, slicing purple onions, anointing the meat with a covert rub, hoisting briskets into pans, wrestling huge slabs of ribs out of Styrofoam coolers, and boiling large pots of beans into which they drop bowling balls of white shortening.

It opened some twenty-five years ago, when Annie Mae accompanied her husband, D.C., on a trip to Huntsville from their Houston home. D.C. came to paint the church, where his mother was a member. Annie Mae came along to keep him company and cook him lunch.

She cooked barbecued chicken right there by the side of the road, and the aroma stopped traffic. Literally. People were getting out of their cars and pleading with her to sell them her husband's chicken.

"He never did get his lunch," Annie Mae explains, her eyes lighting up. "I was barbecuing for him, but I had in mind that something else would happen . . . and it did. You could see all those chickens cooking and my husband can't eat but half of one." Indeed, that day he didn't get to eat any.

She stood out there in her bare feet, cooking and selling every Friday and Saturday while D.C. painted. She expanded the menu. He finished the job, but the barbecue business was so good they decided to up and move to Huntsville.

As a constant traffic jam developed around her little roadside barbecue, the local health inspector took notice, telling Annie Mae that if she wanted to sell cooked meat it had to be indoors, so she moved her operation into the little church annex it's in today.

It's a bit of a shack, as every good barbecue joint rightfully should be. Pilgrims are drawn to this unassuming temple (perhaps along the order of what the Vatican might look like if Jesus were still in charge) in Huntsville from throughout Walker County, the state of Texas, all over the United States, and lately the world. In this way it is like Lourdes, except instead of healing, barbecue probably kills you — as all the best-tasting foods are said to do these days. It's how I want to go.

For the first two years she was in business, Annie Mae gave all proceeds to the church. Now she keeps a little something for herself. "I told the pastor of the church the Lord don't expect me to work this hard for nothing," she says.

Annie Mae's barbecue was a godsend to the little church, the old wooden one D.C. painted. With proceeds from the barbecue it was built anew in brick, to last, and redecorated. There are about twenty worshippers in attendance the Sunday we are there. Annie Mae is decked out in her Sunday best, a blue suit and a red hat, and she makes the weekly announcements about Bible study and choir practice.

On an ordinary weekday, pretty near lunchtime, folks begin arriving from as far as 150 miles away, by car, by truck, by a car on a flatbed truck, by motorcycle, and on foot — all coming to see for themselves if tales of the miraculous barbecue are true.

Is it true you have the best barbecue in Texas? "Yes, it is," Annie Mae answers, and goes back to work. She says, "That ain't braggin', just statin' a fact."

The hungry are greeted by an old sign outside the front door with movable letters spelling out GOD BLESS YI KEEP YOU THANK YOU.

A line forms at the counter. There is an air of anticipation, even among those who come here religiously. This is more than lunch; this is a life experience. The menu is on the wall, carrying a biblical verse from Colossians 3:17, then listing the sacraments: brisket, ribs, links, chicken, potato salad, beans, pickle, onion slice, bread. All you can eat for eight bucks. A BBQ sandwich is three dollars; pecan or potato pie, an extra ninety cents; drinks, fifty cents. No beer, not at the Baptist barbecue. There's ice tea made from a presweetened mix, then spiked with a shovel of sugar. There really ought to be syringes of insulin at the fixins bar. Here, Coke is the healthy beverage choice. Two slices of very white, nutrition-free bread wrapped in clear plastic are at each place setting on the tables.

Annie Mae, a small woman, slight but strong, is in constant motion, taking orders at the counter, carefully counting out change at the cash register, picking up orders, and ladling on a little sauce before delivering the wrist-snapping plates of meat in glistening hues of burnt orange, gold, and brown with touches of black. The portions appear appropriate for the Texas Longhorns football team training table, but turn out to be merely orders for two — refillable. Sometimes, Annie Mae sings softly while she works: "This little light of mine, I'm gonna let it shine."

It's pretty much praise the Lord and pass the ribs once she sets down the platters of barbecue. People fall silent before it. All manner of people are here to partake: students from Sam Houston State University and white-haired retirees; businessmen in suits and laborers in legitimately torn jeans; uniformed prison guards; white people, black people, brown people; people who've arrived by Cadillac and Kia; and people speaking English and Spanish.

Such is the miraculous power of "Q," the power to bring together, in one place, people of all faiths, political beliefs, colors, ethnic groups, incomes, and classes — like nothing and nowhere else I can think of in our thoroughly niched nation. The barbecue-ists sit elbow to elbow, bound together in communal worship.

There is genuine passion here; Mel Gibson could make a movie about barbecue. It's soulful. Something of a religious experience, but more concrete and requiring more napkins. And you can carry out.

Many must. Annie Mae expanded the place to about fifty folding chairs, but it's still not big enough. "On Saturdays you may not get in here," she cautions. In this way it is like the Four Seasons in New York.

The Reverend Clinton J. Edison, pastor of the church, is with us today, bearing a look of transcendence as he dines. "I do pray for Sister Ward," he says, wiping his chin, "and for her barbecue. What makes it so good? It could be divine intervention.

"This is the only church around that feeds you physically as well as spiritually," he says. "You don't hear about all the people that eat here and don't have a dime. Her heart is just so big and she's so dedicated. She's one of the hardest-working people I know of any age."

Mind if I ask your age, Annie Mae? "Yes, I do," she replies, "but I'll answer. Next Thursday I'll be eighty-four. People ask me when I'm gonna retire." She says her retirement plan is to be carried out of the restaurant feet-first, because "this is my love."

One question she won't answer: What's the secret? "There is no secret," she says, adamantly. No secret wood? No secret meat?

No secret sauce? "No, no secrets," she says, with a little smile. "We just don't tell anybody. I just cook it to taste like I want it to taste."

So what is it? Many have tried to divine the answer. No doubt, some large foods conglomerate has taken her barbecue back to the lab for analysis.

But the secret, of course, is Annie Mae.

Barbecue is — unofficially, of course — the official food of rural America. Probably not the official *cuisine*. That would be meat loaf.

Sure, there are great BBQ restaurants in cities — Arthur Bryant's in Kansas City, the Rendezvous in Memphis — but virtually all were started by transplanted country folk. Those that weren't tend to be ersatz BBQs that have been "themed" by throwing vaguely farmy old yard-sale junk up on the walls and a tsunami of sauce on the baked ribs. Many serve nouvelle BBQ in the tradition of the McRib, a product that looks as though it was extracted from a die-cast mold, machine-tooled in Toledo, and coated with thick maroon spray paint. It's like eating part of your dashboard, probably manufactured at the same plant.

A classy restaurant group spent millions of dollars to open the chic Blue Smoke barbecue in Manhattan. Their barbecue is good, but merlot is present as is smoked foie gras, and a rib dinner will cost you about forty bucks. (To be fair, if the ribs were cheaper, New Yorkers wouldn't order them.)

Like rural people themselves, BBQ is unpretentious and indeed downright *anti*-pretentious. That's part of the reason we like it. Barbecue joints tend not to have sommeliers or valet parking or table-cloths.

You don't have to worry about which knife, fork, or spoon to use when there ain't none. At two world-renowned BBQs, the Kreuz Market and Smitty's, both in Lockhart, Texas (pop: 11,615), there's no silverware, not even plates — plastic or otherwise. Smitty's serves smoked meat and only smoked meat, no sides, on sheets of butcher paper. Without sauce. The flavor comes from dry rub and smoke.

When you're finished, you need a roll of paper towels and a hot shower. This flavorful, greasy, messy all-American food is to be consumed with a general disregard for table manners and health concerns.

Like all religions, barbecue has many denominations that squabble over which is best: North Carolina or Texas? Kansas City or Memphis? Wet or dry? Beef or pork? Chopped, sliced, or pulled? Slaw on the sandwiches or slaw off?

But certain tenets are held by most sects. There really ought to be an alarming amount of smoke pouring from a good barbecue restaurant, enough to set off smoke detectors for miles around. Ideally a good BBQ joint is a little out of the way and small, although they can be too small. We stopped at Spooney's, a sliver of a spot in downtown, if you will, Greenwood, Mississippi, where the sole employee (Spooney?) took our order then ran out the back door to buy charcoal and meat at the store. Hadn't been expecting a lunch crowd of four.

Whenever possible, the restaurant should be a slightly run-down shanty, not a hygienic new structure — although Kreuz Market is an old spot that moved into a newly constructed building when the proprietor's sister raised the rent, forced her brother out, and opened her own BBQ, Smitty's, in the old building. The banished brother ceremoniously carried coals from the fire down the road to his new location.

Ambiance — just another form of flavor — counts. I think the best barbecue I ever had was at the Salt Lick, in Driftwood, Texas (pop: 21), where people wait to get in for an hour or more, sitting outside at picnic tables socializing and drinking beer from their coolers. They bring the coolers inside with them when they're finally seated, and will even toss a stranger a cool one if you ask neighborly-like.

In Tennessee, my son took me out in the boondocks to a joint where folks ate barbecue and drank harmful intoxicants from Ball jars. It was a former gas station — converted after the owner started barbecuing in an underutilized repair bay, selling the fare through a hole he punched in the wall. As business picked up, customers brought tables and chairs so they could sit down, and pretty soon musicians from Nashville came out to play in return for barbecue and whatever that was in those Ball jars. It was a great barbecue experience, although I don't remember much about the food.

Frozen Dead Guy

NEDERLAND, COLORADO, POP: 1,337

The air's a bit thin up in Nederland, Colorado (elev: 8,234), which may help explain things.

Everything's a little different in this quaint mountain hamlet just fifteen miles or so straight up from Boulder, but a good deal further out. It's a place where there was something of an uproar when police began actually enforcing drug and alcohol laws; a place where everything — food, clothing, shelter, health care — tends toward the "alternative." The wellness center boasts that all its electricity is wind-generated (best to cancel that heart bypass if it's a calm day), its computers low-megahertz (typewriters?), and its toilets ultra-low-flush (outside?).

Formerly a town of roughneck miners, cowboys, and loggers, today it's populated by a lot of former hippies, eccentrics, and staunch individualists. Whenever another young professional moves in, one who probably commutes to Boulder or even Denver, the locals see it as further evidence that their unique little town is going to hell in a handbasket.

So perhaps it's not surprising that their annual festival is a little different too, honoring not a local fruit or vegetable or their ethnic heritage, but rather a dead man kept on ice in a backyard shed here. It's Frozen Dead Guy Days!

"I support anything that keeps Nederland unique," says a woman who runs an all-organic bakery for dogs, something one rarely finds in small towns, and she seems to speak for the majority.

"Who's the frozen dead guy?" festivalgoers from out of town ask at the Frozen Dead Guy Days Information Center.

Well, it seems that one Trygve Bauge (Trig-VAH BOW-gay) moved from Norway to Nederland, where he fit in nicely with the local new-age lifestyle, promoting wellness through regular immersions in icy water. He held the world record for bathing in ice water: one hour and four minutes.

Trygve was a firm believer in cryogenics, freezing bodies after death, which in coldest, darkest Norway is really not all that different from life when you think about it. So when his grandfather, Bredo Morstoel, died in Norway in 1989, Trygve had him frozen solid and flown to Los Angeles, where he was kept at a modern cryogenics facility.

That got expensive, plus Trygve wanted to start his own cryogenics business, so he had Grandpa flown to Denver, where he and his friend, Walter, picked him up in a station wagon at the airport. He couldn't very well catch a cab.

"I thought it was a shipment of frozen shrimp," explains Walter, who Trygve did not tell otherwise. Walter said he was not surprised when he found out it was Grandpa, because "with Trygve one doesn't get surprised anymore."

Not having the venture capital to build a high-tech, state-of-the-art liquid-nitrogen cryogenic facility, Trygve put Bredo in a toolshed behind his house and covered him with ice. (Hey, it works for Swanson Hungry Man Salisbury steak dinners.)

Using Grandpa as a loss-leader, Trygve hoped to attract more bodies, and sure enough the late Al Campbell arrived from Chicago and went into the shed. Little is known of Al's circumstances except that he was dead.

Sure, it was a pain keeping Bredo and Al on ice, but friends like Walter pitched in to help. When Trygve had to leave town, he'd ask a friend or neighbor if they'd mind icing down Grandpa, much as you'd ask someone to water your plants or feed the fish.

This worked fine for five years, then Trygve was snatched by the Immigration and Naturalization Service for having an expired visa and deported. Among other things, Trygve had been arrested for joking about hijacking a plane at the Denver airport, and the INS didn't really seem to like him. His mother, Aud, was living with him at the time in his yet-to-be-completed, disaster-proof concrete home. She told authorities that she could probably manage for herself without Trygve, but was concerned about the continued care and cooling of the bodies in the toolshed.

"Bodies! What bodies?" whelps filmmaker Kathy Beeck, describing the town's panic attack.

"Everybody went nuts!"

Sirens wailed. Headlines screamed: BODIES FOUND ON ICE, TWO FROZEN CORPSES DISCOVERED AT HOME OF POLAR BEAR — a reference to Trygve being the founding member of the local Polar Bear swim club.

66

Clay Evans, a new night-beat reporter on *The Daily Camera* newspaper, broke the big story. Did it shock him that someone would have bodies in the backyard? "Not particularly," he says. "This is a different kind of town. It's not a coincidence that this story happened here."

"You might find it strange if you don't live here," explains a spokesman for the Chamber of Commerce, "but if you live here it's not strange."

After the initial panic, the town council quickly passed an ordinance against having a frozen dead relative in a shed behind your house, which sounds pretty darned restrictive to me.

"We will move the body when we want," Aud, Trygve's mom, defiantly proclaimed. "I will fight until I am president of this country!" But, alas, her platform seemed too narrowly defined and her campaign never really caught fire. She was deported.

Al Campbell was asked to leave, and although dead, moved back to Chicago. But Nederlanders were having a change of heart about Bredo, one of whom told the town council, "He's the best neighbor I've got." You can't borrow a cup of sugar from him, but he doesn't hold loud parties or keep broken-down major appliances on his porch, either.

67

The frozen Bredo was hailed as "a champion for the rights of the temporarily dead" by Robin Beeck, a filmmaker who made a documentary with her sisters about this surreal saga, *Grandpa's Still in the Tuff Shed* (Tuff Shed being the brand name of Grandpa's tin mausoleum). "The film is about love, death, ice, and high hopes," Robin explains. "It's not really about a dead body. It's about how a town came together. At first they were saying, 'Oh my God we can't have this, it's gonna taint the water supply,' 'Send in a hazmat team,' 'Get that body out of here,' and then the town came together. They came to the board and said, 'You know what? We want to let him stay.'"

The council voted to allow Grandpa to be "grandfathered" in as a preexisting use. GRANDPA TO BE LEFT WHERE HE IS trumpeted a local paper. The Tuff Shed company donated a new, sturdier storage unit. Local residents helped construct it. Someone delivered eight hundred pounds of ice.

Why, if it weren't so damned creepy, it would almost be heartwarming. Bredo had gone from being a heinous health hazard to . . . well, if he isn't the Chamber of Commerce "Man of the Year," I don't know who is.

Frozen Dead Guy Days draws thousands of people every March, who park in Frozen

Dead Guy lots, buy Frozen Dead Guy hats and T-shirts at the Frozen Dead Guy Tourist Information Center, and attend Frozen Dead Guy activities.

There's the Frozen Dead Guy parade, featuring vintage hearses, grim reaper outfits, and decorated coffins that are later carried by teams of pallbearers over a snowy mogul course in the coffin races. And there's the Polar Plunge, where participants run across an ice-covered pond in their swimsuits and jump into a hole cut in the ice. This event was started by Trygve, who advocated health and well-being through icy baths and coffee enemas. Luckily, event planners chose icy baths this year.

There's a Grandpa Bredo look-alike contest in the venerable Pioneer Inn bar, where revelers guzzle Dead Guy Ale. The contest winner is local long-bearded personality Toasty Post, whose name hints at his drinking habits and who looks like the lost ZZ Top triplet. The evening brings Grandpa's Blue Ball, where townspeople dance to Chip and the Chowderheads belting out that instant classic "Grandpa's in the Tuff Shed":

Grandpa's in the Tuff Shed, lying all alone; Grandpa's in the Tuff Shed, chillin' to the bone . . .

And so on.

Next morning, Frozen Dead Guy tours are departing regularly from the Frozen Dead Guy center. Normally, the price to see Grandpa is $25, but they're running a Dead Guy festival special: two for the price of one.

We board the 10:30 van for a ride up the hill, where Grandpa's current ice-provider and entrepreneur, Bo Shaffer, greets us.

"Welcome to the Life Extension Institute," Bo says, referring to the concrete shell of what was to have been Trygve's disaster-proof (atom bombs, earthquakes, fire, tornadoes) home. Rumor has it that the property is on the market but proving to be a tough sell, owing to the absence of plumbing or electricity — and the corpse in the backyard.

"And this is the cryonic storage facility," says Bo, walking to the Tuff Shed, emblazoned with THE FOX in huge red letters, representing the Denver radio station that raised funds for Grandpa's maintenance. A good cause. Bo, who describes himself as an "environmental consultant and planetary ecologist," opens the two large front doors on the shed, which is roughly about eight feet high, eight feet deep, and ten feet wide.

Unfortunately — or perhaps not — you don't see Bredo himself but rather a plywood sarcophagus, or box, which Bo opens to reveal about a ton of dry ice. Grandpa is said to be under the ice in a chained and padlocked stainless steel casket. In there with him is a piece of his 101st birthday cake for him to enjoy when he and it are thawed.

Still, tourists think they got their money's worth. "Fascinating," says a man from Ohio. "I've been laughing ever since I've been here," says a woman from Kansas, perhaps inappropriately, adding: "If there's a lesson to be learned it's tell your relatives your burial plans before you die."

"We don't consider Grandpa Bredo to be dead," says Bo, correcting her. "We're keeping him in a state that someday will allow us to reanimate him." He says reanimation occurs when a cure is found for whatever killed you, although this would seem to be more feasible with diseases than, say, a head-on collision with a semi. But I'm no cryogenicist.

Appropriate refreshments are served. There's a bottle of Old Grand-Dad bourbon on top of the plywood box next to Bredo's framed photograph, and several of us toast him and take a swig.

Then we're herded into the gift shop, where all tours come to an end. "Last but not least, for your souvenir pleasure," Bo announces, "we offer you a piece of Grandpa's

71

original shed, complete with a certificate of authenticity ($4 upgrade), all for the nominal fee of fifteen dollars." I know a deal when I see it, so I snapped that up, but passed on the $5 photographs autographed somehow by Bredo himself.

Things are working out so well with the festival that some have suggested bringing in more frozen stiffs. "But the neighbors were like, 'You know I think one stiff grandpopsicle is enough,' " Robin says. Yet the Bredo phenomenon grows, now featuring Grandpa ghost sightings.

Trygve is paying Bo $650 a month to keep Grandpa on ice, but many here worry that Bredo may never be revivified. "I've been told by experts that he would have been far better off in liquid nitrogen," Walter says.

"He's actually defrosted three times," says Robin.

"To say it very simply," says Gordon, a friend of Walter's, "freezer burn may very well have set in."

But, you know, even if Trygve Bauge's low-tech cryogenics attempt proves unsuccessful, Grandpa Bredo has already achieved a kind of immortality.

To get to these remote villages across the country I fly a lot. And if I believed the old adage that "getting there is half the fun" I'd shoot myself or eat airline food or do

Annie Mae Ward at the Church of the Holy BBQ

something almost as drastic. There's airport security, which treats old ladies in wheelchairs like Mohamed Atta and makes you want to show up wearing a clear plastic shower curtain; ram-

Gay Balfour out doggin'

pant delays caused by, say, relatively high humidity; less space on-board than legally required for transporting livestock — it all adds up.

Elsie Eiler, the population of Monowi, Nebraska

I have had good flights, however, and one great one, a flight I call "First Class to Vegas," something of a contradiction in terms. I received an up-

The author with Hal on his paper route

grade when a seat opened up because Don King hadn't made the flight. The first-class cabin was filled with Mike Tyson and Don King's entourage headed for a prizefight. The drinking began before the cabin door closed and most in the group were aloft before the plane.

Somewhere over Lake Michigan, a raucous limbo contest broke out in the aisle. A publicist began signing Mike Tyson's name to 8x10 glossies of the champ, and when a passenger expressed surprise, he slurred, "Who the hell did you think signs Mike Tyson's pictures?"

Also up front was a man whose wife was sitting back in coach, and she came forward looking rather perturbed that he was having such a high old time. A stewardess was making out with a guy in the galley! It turned out not to be the pilot, as I feared, but her boyfriend. Recognizing a Code Blue when he saw it, another flight attendant announced that the plane had completely run out of alcoholic beverages, which is possible but has to be an FAA violation of some kind. Next to me was a tough-talking guy from Jersey who said he was in the "cartage business" (aka cold-blooded killing). When it was announced we were approaching Las Vegas, he sat bolt upright, grabbed his camera, and snapped a flash picture of the total blackness outside his window.

As uncomfortable as flying can be these days, it normally doesn't qualify you for a Purple Heart, although there are exceptions. On a flight that never took off, we sat on the tarmac for two hours until the flight was canceled. The instant we arrived back at the gate a fellow traveler sprang to his feet, popped open the overhead, and jerked out his (blunt) briefcase, which hit me on the top of the head, cracked my head open, and caused a geyser of blood to come gushing out. The culprit hightailed it, glancing back not out of concern but rather to make sure no one was gaining on him.

Medical personnel came aboard, wrapped my head in bandages, from top to chin, and took a detailed report. I don't know how they got my number, but the next day two concerned passengers called me: a woman who'd sat next to me to ask if I had AIDS, and a fellow across the aisle to ask if he could represent me in a lawsuit. I thanked him for his kindness, but explained that I considered lawyers like himself to be slime-sucking scam artists. And I assured the woman I did not have AIDS, just a touch of Ebola.

I've not been involved in an airline accident,

except one time when my plane was backing out of a gate and hit another plane. Captain! Use those side mirrors. There have been some near accidents. Five minutes after one takeoff a flight attendant announced that the lavatories were not functioning. An elderly man sitting next to me shouted, "What if someone has diarrhea?" Everyone turned around to see who'd asked the question. I shook my head to let everyone know it wasn't me. I hoped it was a rhetorical question, not one that he'd answer in some nonverbal way. And he posed a follow-up question to the nearest rows, "What if someone ate soft foods for lunch?" That puzzled me.

A flight attendant stopped by to ask those of us in the exit row if we felt we were capable of opening the emergency door if need be. I told her that I was, but the fellow in the window seat next to me was Korean, spoke no English, and had no idea what she was saying. "Door," she said, pointing to it. "Can . . . you . . . open?" He finally understood, nodded his head, and grabbed the door handle. "No! No! Not now!" she screamed.

I've had some dreamy flights: on a blimp drifting over Miami on a sunny sixty-degree January day, low and slow, with the windows open;

in an open-cockpit biplane over the breathtaking Maine coast; in a seaplane that landed on its belly in the waters off Key West; and in a helicopter landing on the helipads of some of the world's largest private yachts. There have been some harrowing flights: in a six-seater through a lightning storm at night over the mountains of North Carolina; and in a light plane that landed on the main street of a small town in Kansas.

There have been some touching moments, too: flying with a young soldier on his way home to Eureka, California, where he was greeted with balloons, cheers, and tears of joy; with a woman holding a tiny baby she was delivering to its new adoptive parents; with a mother who poured her heart out about the tragic death of her son, and who had become a flight attendant at age forty-seven so she could fly with her daughter, a flight attendant.

Tips for Travelers: Signs You May Be Having A Bad Flight Experience

1. You receive airline's first-ever downgrade . . . from coach to all-new DIRT class (Downright Inhumane Rude Treatment)
2. When checking bags, agent asks if you'd like a moment to kiss them goodbye
3. TSA agent Tasers you for carrying unau-

thorized toothpaste and shaving cream — a potentially lethal combination . . .

4. . . . as six swarthy men in "Al Qaeda Flight School Picnic" T-shirts are waved through
5. TSA agent pats you down very thoroughly and slips you his phone number
6. Heightened security on this Keokuk–Cedar Rapids flight due to rumors terrorists have targeted the Dairy Queen
7. Flight delayed three hours due to partly cloudiness
8. Pilot boards wearing WWI ace leather cap, goggles, scarf, and jacket lettered "Howdy's Aerial Stunt Circus"
9. Copilot boards carrying "roadie" from Sky Hi airport bar
10. Flight attendants uniformed in brown shirts and black leather boots, brandishing riding crops
11. Yours is a center seat, back row, between sumo tag-team partners
12. Everything in coach is extra: $5 drink charge . . . $20 for seat belts . . . $25,000 for emergency oxygen
13. Charged $5 for headset to watch movie, *Syriana;* in coach, George Clooney's Oscar-winning role is played by Richard Simmons

14. Tow truck arrives to jump-start plane
15. Pilot kneels down next to you with map and asks, "How would you go?"
16. Captain comes on intercom, talks at length about inclement weather and his recent bouts of depression, and says the flight may be touching down a lot earlier than scheduled
17. Passenger in front of you reclines seat, embedding tray table in your solar plexus
18. Plane leaves gate, but sits on tarmac for two hours before takeoff; sky marshall begins playing Russian roulette
19. Meal is bag of Deluxe Party Mix containing two peanuts and five pieces of what appears to be packing material
20. Meal is "Airplane 'Chicken,'" specially bred for the airlines by DuPont's roofing and siding division, Polyfowl
21. Pilot makes emergency landing in Nova Scotia when you attempt to use first-class toilet . . .
22. . . . but not before you discover they have real toilet tissue up there rather than the old *SkyMall* magazine they give you in coach
23. Guy across the aisle cursing loudly because he can't light his damned shoes (apparently there are no Boy Scouts in

Saudi Arabia)
24. Pilot, bored after one hour in holding pattern, does a series of loop-de-loops
25. Pilot announces: "We'll be landing shortly in . . . San Antonio? Damn!"

THE LAND OF
LOST LUGGAGE!

SCOTTSBORO, ALABAMA, POP: 14,762

Millions of bags are checked at airports every day, thousands of which are never to be seen again.

But where do they go? Oddly enough, almost all flock to the same destination: a remote village in the Appalachian foothills where indigenous peoples celebrate the misfortunes of air travelers, enjoying deep discounts on their losses in . . . The Land of Lost Luggage!

I'd heard tales of this mysterious locale, but figured it for folklore, until I saw it with my own eyes: the Unclaimed Baggage Center in Scottsboro, Alabama, an orphanage of sorts for virtually all lost bags. But despair not. Here, your luggage and its contents will find good homes.

In Scottsboro, they call luggage lost by the airlines "unclaimed baggage," as though it was you who flew to the wrong place (Kansas City), and not your bags (Kuala Lumpur). As though you hadn't waited in vain at the luggage carousel, staring with growing desperation at that black hole up-chucking the bags of the lucky ones. As though you hadn't waited around half the day to see if your luggage might be on the next flight, then filled out all the paperwork, stopped at a 7-Eleven to buy a toothbrush, and made a dozen fruitless calls to the air-line, spending hours on hold listening to in-strumental versions of "Feelings." As though you hadn't attended your friend's out-of-town wedding in the "Let's Go Mets" T-shirt you wore on the plane.

Or maybe it's the bags' fault. The airlines like to say a bag "fails to make a flight," or they'll call it "mishandled baggage," as in "a small percentage of the two billion bags checked every year are mishandled."

But how, and why, on earth does your Samsonite or American Tourister end up in a small town in northeastern Alabama? Well, for openers, it's not yours anymore. Bryan Owens, owner of the United Baggage Center (UBC), buys your lost luggage from the airlines after they've "tried" unsuccessfully for about ninety days to reunite you and your bag. (Can't you see a TV show where Maury Povich reunites lost suitcases with their tearful owners?)

Bryan, a dapper middle-aged businessman, buys the bags by the pound or yard, sight unseen. They arrive in a steady flow of trailer trucks at the UBC, where they're opened and the contents sorted, some of it going to charity, some to the cleaners, some directly onto store shelves. "We stock seven thousand never-seen-before items in the store every day," Bryan says, carefully avoiding the word "new." "We throw out the pornography and liquor," he says. Where?

The idea of benefiting from the losses of others is as old as morticians and pawnbrokers, as fresh as personal injury lawyers and television newscasters, but what ingenious, entrepreneurial mind came up with this idea?

"My father, Doyle, started the business in 1970," Bryan recalls, "with a borrowed pickup truck and a $300 loan, and he was off to buy his first load of unclaimed bags. From buses. We had a few card tables set up and had clothes dumped on the tables and sold them that way." An industry was born, a monopoly.

No more card tables. The UBC is a vast, modern department store on the order of, say, a Target. But with better stuff: Prada, Tiffany, Hermès, Dolce & Gabbana, Evan Picone, Dior, Gucci — just a few of the designer tags I notice on a wide variety of items that, while not new and not available in a variety of sizes, are half the price of new. "People tend to take their best things on trips," notes Bryan, who happens to be wearing someone else's Cartier wristwatch.

"You just don't find things like this in stores in northeastern Alabama, trust me," says one knowledgeable consumer. Lost luggage is a planetary problem and Bryan buys it the world over. "Exotic international outfits," says another shopper, "from Africa to India to China." Where to wear them in northeastern Alabama is your problem.

And the UBC is way more interesting than your normal stores. Along with the thousands of clothing items, digital cameras, stereos, books, perfumes, golf clubs, rugs (Oriental to purple shag), and other relatively standard fare, you come across some of the damnedest things imaginable, and unimaginable. Who takes a kitchen faucet on a plane trip? Who loses a full-size Windsurfer? An ornate, double-decked, carved wood Greek Orthodox church table? A ten-foot Swiss Alps horn? Major appliances: a TV, a clothes dryer? Who leaves behind their wheelchair? Was there a faith healer on board?

You hope the musician who lost the trumpet wasn't on his way to a gig. You hope the tuba being tested by a customer to the delight of fellow shoppers wasn't lost on the way to wherever tuba players go. Likewise, the accordion. I tried to play "Stars Fell on Alabama" and "Sweet Home Alabama" on a mishandled didgeridoo, accompanied by two other shoppers on the lost maracas . . . but we saw early on we weren't going anywhere, so the group broke up.

You hope the woman (presumably) who lost her Las Vegas showgirl outfit — bra, bikini bottoms, headpiece, all encrusted with hundreds of multicolored glass jewels — was able to run out to a local department store and replace it.

And you sincerely hope the many brides who lost their wedding dresses were on their way home from the ceremonies. God! Those baggage handlers should do hard time, seriously. The $2,500 maximum payment per lost bag just doesn't cut it.

"We open up these bags and never know what we'll find," Bryan says. "Every day is like Christmas around here." They might find another glass eye, perhaps another mummified falcon, another $17,000 diamond necklace. "It's a bit like an archaeological dig. It's a cross-section of what's going on in society. You open up a bag, you know what the most popular novels are, what the current fashions are, what kind of electronic gizmos people are carrying with them. You can tell a lot about the society by what people pack." Bryan says there are some big surprises and absolute shocks. "We opened up one bag packed full of Egyptian artifacts dating back to 1500 BC; we had a camera designed for the space shuttle; an F-16 guidance system; a six-carat diamond solitaire ring worth about $20,000; a huge emerald, forty-one carats, so big we didn't think it could be real."

An original oil painting was sold here for $50 and later appraised at $20,000. "We missed that one," Bryan says. "Another customer bought a suitcase, tossed it in her attic, and a couple of years later pulled it out and found $2,000 in a little side pouch."

Most shoppers come for lesser goods, least of all the half-used lipsticks and other people's underpants. Gross. "We have the largest cleaning and dry-cleaning facility in the area," Bryan assures us. Still . . .

And there's a popular new line: prohibited

items confiscated from air travelers by Transportation Security Administration agents. Bryan buys these too. "We get in fingernail clippers, nail files, and knives almost by the ton. Tear gas, firearms." Yes, the UBC has all your weaponry needs.

Do they ever try to reunite the items with their rightful owners? Nope. It's finders keepers, losers weepers. Do the losers ever come here seeking their own lost stuff? Yes, but they never seem to find it, although strange things do happen.

"I was looking at a painting," says Rob, a customer, "and I immediately recognized the subject as a hot air balloon owned by a friend of mine. I bought it, delivered it to my friend and his wife, and they started crying. It turned out the painting was done by their daughter, who was in art school in Los Angeles and lost the painting at LAX. She was crushed. It was a Christmas gift to her parents. It's a little mystical, don't you think?"

Ron said his neighbor here in Scottsboro left a new blazer on a flight, and when the UBC sorters recognized his name inside the jacket they called him. Wonder if he had to buy it back? And there's the tale of the man who bought ski boots here for his wife and she found her maiden name inscribed inside the boots, which had been lost on a flight years ago.

Other towns are built on the steel industry, or autos, or crops, or music, or computer technology. Lost luggage has made this rather poor little town on the Tennessee River a major tourist destination attracting way more visitors than they get over at NASA's Space and Rocket Center in Huntsville. The UBC has a coffee shop, a souvenir stand, and a concierge to answer questions like where to spend the night and where there's a golf course he can play while she shops. Lost luggage mini-vacations!

The UBC claims a million shoppers a year, a figure that may be distorted somewhat by A. Z. Proctor, a retiree who comes to the UBC three times a day. "You'd be surprised what some people take with them on planes," he says.

Allan Garner, another shopper, has been coming three to four times a week for thirty years. "I like stuff that's broken in," he says. "You go buy something new and you're gonna mess it up so why not buy something already messed up?" Follow?

He's seen some highly unusual items come and go. "I remember when Jesse Jackson was running for president his suits came in here. Had his name in them. And one time when

88

MC Hammer was touring his backdrop came in here from his concert stage." (Lost cargo comes here too.) Great buy, but tough to blend into your home decor I would think.

Scottsboro, Alabama, is an entire town dressed in other people's stuff, which doesn't really seem to bother them all that much.

Do any of them ever feel like, I don't know, vultures? Nope. "Sometimes I think about it and I feel sorry for them that they lost it," says Marilyn, a regular shopper at UBC, "but since it's already lost, it's OK. I haven't had any nightmares, you know?"

One person's loss is another's gain. I watch a teenage girl, a fair-skinned redhead, excitedly admire a red dress, a bejeweled sheath — what you'd call a cocktail dress or a prom dress if she were old enough for either.

"It's so beautiful!" she cries.

"Where you gonna wear it?" cautions Mom.

"Can I at least try it on?" she pleads with her mother, who refers her to Dad, who says it's probably OK to just go ahead and try it.

"It's so beautiful Mom, look at it," says the infatuated daughter. "I'd be so unhappy if I'd lost this. She must have been going someplace really special."

The girl goes into the changing room and

emerges . . . changed . . . suddenly looking grown-up, beautiful . . . and she's beaming. Her parents seem a bit taken aback by the sight.

Here in Scottsboro, what's lost is found, and the unhappiness of loss gives way to the joy of a fourteen-year-old girl who bought her first evening dress with her lawn-mowing money, for $12, in . . . The Land of Lost Luggage!

RED RAILS IN THE SUNSET

HANLONTOWN, IOWA, POP: 229

People are always telling me they'd love to drive coast-to-coast someday, New York to L.A., and really *see* America. Having done it, I always suggest they consider flying from New York to Denver and driving the spectacular rest of the way. Maybe skip a thousand miles or so of cornfields; an hour of 'em pretty much gives you the idea.

But then you'd miss places like Hanlontown, Iowa, a tiny dot on the map hidden away in the midst of all that corn, a spot you might not even notice driving through unless there was a tractor in front of you holding things up. When you see the sign, you'd better hit the brakes hard or you're in Fertile. You'd think Hanlontown's population would

91

grow, situated as it is between Manly and Fertile, but alas. Hanlontown, like a lot of small burgs in America, had been trying to come up with something about itself to celebrate by way of a festival, or a museum, or maybe a gussied-up birthplace of some semi-important somebody or other, something that might draw free-spending city dwellers, whose dollars are worth a lot less to them where they come from than dollars are to folks in small-town America.

Often these little towns don't have a lot to work with to attract tourism. And no budget to hire a public relations firm to sort of, you know, make something up. (Gateway to Southwest North Dakota?) Not to mention, it kind of goes against the grain of rural folk to embellish the facts or to toot their own horns, even in truth.

So the ideas small towns come up with to attract visitors are often simple, honest, unsophisticated, and, not surprisingly, corny. Hanlontown had already tried Pork Days, a typical rural festival where folks admire pigs, give them ribbons — then eat them. And what finer compliment?

"How'd that go over?" I ask a man on the street (in fact, the *only* man on the street) in Hanlontown. "Fair," he answers, although his tone of voice makes it sound more like "fair-to-poor." Small-town Midwesterners don't like to understate or overstate. That's what makes them better people and worse interviews.

The problem with Pork Days seemed to be that lots of towns in the Midwest hold them. There's a huge celebration of the "Other White Meat" at World Pork Expo in Des Moines, which I've attended. (I'm not bragging, it's open to the public.)

Folks in Hanlontown wanted to celebrate something — but what? The "downtown" has a newly reopened café (The Neighbor's Place), a nice water tower, some good-size grain silos across the road, a nice old bank building that's closed, and a train that doesn't stop here anymore.

But wait! The *tracks* are still there. "So what?" you say. Well, get this: every June 21, on the summer solstice, the sun sets smack-dab in the center of the train tracks. "And?" you may ask. Well, maybe folks would come to see *that!*

Hanlontown gave it a whirl. They named their festival Sundown Days, printed up some T-shirts, and put on a schedule of dazzling events: an antique tractor parade, a tractor pull, a kids' peddle-toy tractor pull, an auction typified by a set of four TV tables going to the highest bidder for $6, a K-3d grade prince and princess pageant held without pageantry in front of the fire station/city hall/library/community center, plus a roving (but not very far) barbershop quartet, despite there being no barbershop.

The year I attend, a lovely, sprightly woman, Rua Doebel, is the parade grand marshal. She was then 101 years old, same age as the town, and in the parade she wears a horned Viking helmet for some reason as she waves from a Viking ship pulled by a tractor. Why, we do not know.

Ms. Doebel says people had noticed for quite some time that the sun set in the middle of the tracks, but nobody ever did anything about it. "We all noticed it, but we didn't pay much attention," she said. "But in the past couple of years, people have drawn attention to it because it attracts people to see if the sun will set in the middle of the tracks. That's funny, isn't it?"

And has the big festival attracted visitors from far and wide? I ask yet another man on the street, as the festival crowd begins to swell into the tens of people.

"No, not really," he says, his wife on the street agreeing: "No I don't think so." And from how far away have they come? "Oh, maybe three miles or five," she thinks.

A few hours before sunset, young Mayor

Rick Scholbrock is upbeat: "There'll probably be fifty, sixty, seventy people out here maybe. There'll be cars lined up on the street here. The tracks just glow. It's really neat. It's hard to describe."

"People get excited about it," says one of his constituents, and most agree, although one man chimes in: "If you like watching cement set." There's always the town curmudgeon.

"We live out in the middle of the corn and bean fields," explains Dan Moretz, "and there's not a whole lot to get excited about, you know?"

Local residents talk of sunsets gone by and pull out their photographs. Clayton Rye has them from a number of years back: a nice one from '89 and a beauty from '82.

But aren't they all pretty much the same? "Hardly," he says. "Clouds spoil a lot of 'em. Look at this one here. It was clear all day until just three minutes before the sun set. And there came that bank of clouds. And '96, '97, '98, '99, all spoiled by clouds. You take your chances."

Clouds! Why didn't we think of that before coming all the way out here? And this day, there are definite cloud concerns. "It doesn't look good so far," says one woman. "There's a little glimpse of it, though. It might get underneath there."

Mayor Scholbrock is also concerned about the clouds, but as a civic leader, he has to stay positive to avoid an outbreak of doom and dismay among the populace on this festive occasion.

"You think it's going to make it out of the clouds?" I ask.

"I hope so," the mayor says privately. "I've sat through rainstorms down at the tracks, and it's pretty disappointing."

Then, almost magically, the sun drops beneath the clouds, just above the horizon, and begins heading for the tracks. The traditional bike ride to the sunset is hastily organized. The mayor always leads a couple of dozen riders, taking a circuitous route to make it last longer. They arrive at the tracks and pretty soon the rest of the town does too. Excitement mounts. "Oh this may be the best one yet!" gushes one man.

My only question is whether the sun is going to make it to the middle of the tracks. I have somehow failed to notice in my first fifty years on earth that the sun drops in the sky at a rather severe, forty-five-degree angle.

I set my folding chair right in between the rails and open a beer. Come to papa!

People stare in awe. Cameras flash.

"Wow!" gasps a woman in the crowd.

The sun nestles slowly onto the rails, causing them to glow as though the blazing fireball was turning them red hot. I can see what all the excitement is about, and can appreciate this small town, where they still take time to enjoy the simple pleasures.

A year later, I'm heading home in Manhattan when I look west and notice the sun setting smack-dab in the middle of Ninety-third Street, between the blocks of buildings and parked cars, turning them a fiery red. I almost point it out to a passerby, but stop myself.

The Home of the Range

GREENWOOD, MISSISSIPPI,
POP: 17,344

Down South, amid the cotton fields of the Mississippi Delta, legend has it that "the grandfather of the blues," Robert Johnson, went down to the crossroads at midnight and traded his soul to the devil for an ungodly talent to play the guitar.

Most believe it happened in Clarksdale at the intersection of Highway 61 and Highway 49; some say it was over in Rosedale, where Highway 8 meets Highway 1; others say it never happened at all.

For those who like their folklore a bit less mystical, a modern-day tale grows about a local boy in the Delta who magically transformed his poor, old, dilapidated hometown into a thriving community of hip, boutique businesses that draws people from all over the country and the world. It happened at the intersection of Highway 82 and Highway 49 in Greenwood, and this one you can see with your own eyes.

The Delta is the capital of cotton, birthplace of the blues, and to the great surprise of many, home of the range — the high-tech, high-style, high-priced Viking range, created, manufactured, and headquartered in the little Mississippi town of Greenwood.

"People are always really surprised to hear that," says Fred Carl Jr., in a soft Southern drawl. "They really are. This sleek, modern product made in Mississippi? Sometimes they'll argue, 'Oh no, they're not made in Mississippi.' There's this image that we can grow cotton and catfish down here and that's about it."

Once a bustling town known as the Cotton Capital of the World, where farmers, brokers, buyers, and shippers met, Greenwood had been in a steady decline for the better part of half a century when Fred, a local builder, came up with the preposterous notion that we the people wanted big, hulking, fire-breathing restaurant ranges in our home kitchens.

Say what?! We were cooking less and eating out more, and when we did cook at home it was usually in the microwave. "That is true," Fred says, shaking his head. "So I guess we were kind of going the opposite way weren't we?" He said it as if none of that had ever occurred to him; and come to think of it, such negative thoughts probably never enter Fred's mind.

Now to me, installing a restaurant stove in your home kitchen seems about as sensible as building a four-story parking garage in your backyard for your two cars. It's just the kind of dumb idea that highly successful entrepreneurs often have.

Fred is a shy, balding man in his fifties who wears round horn-rimmed glasses, a neatly trimmed white beard, and rumpled khakis. He was a building contractor whose wife, Margaret, and a couple of clients, mentioned that they wished they could get big, powerful old stoves like their grandmothers used to have. They don't make those anymore, so what they were talking about were really restaurant stoves that without firewalls, tons of insulation, and commercial venting systems burn down your house.

But Fred tried drawing designs for a restaurant-style home stove on the back of scraps of paper for a year and a half, and when he had one he liked he started showing it around. Retailers told him that no one in their right mind would pay $3,000, $4,000, or $5,000 for a stove when they could get a good GE for $300. He took his idea to all the major stove manufacturers. "They laughed and sent me on my way," Fred recalls. "What I got was a lot of noes."

But, as Margaret could have told these naysayers, Fred does not take "no" for an answer. When they were in high school, her parents said Fred was too old to date her, so he paid a younger boy a six-pack of beer to pick her up for him — for two years. A week after she turned eighteen, Fred and Margaret were married.

While piling up rejections on his stove idea, Fred was also sending out flyers to thousands of kitchen designers. But would anyone want such a monster in their home?

Well, yes, one anyway: Patricia King, of Greenwich Village in New York. When her architect told her that a restaurant stove would take up half her new kitchen with all the required fire safety impedimenta, she said, "There has to be something between an ordinary stove and a huge restaurant range." The architect replied that, unfortunately, there was not, then happened upon one of Fred's flyers.

"I was the first person to buy a Viking range," says Pat. "In fact, when I ordered my first Viking range I don't think there was a Viking range yet." She put down a $100 deposit on the wildly expensive $3,000 stove, not realizing that not one had ever been built and that Viking had two unpaid employees, one of them Fred.

Down in Greenwood, Fred had to scramble. A prototype was built in 1986 and shipped to Pat a full nine months later. It was a disaster. Fred dispatched local repairmen in New York to fix Pat's stove on numerous occasions, and once flew in a team from Greenwood.

Eventually they made it work, and Pat was thrilled. She says people came from far and wide to see her range, "and I just knew I wasn't the only one who wanted one." Right she was. Word spread among kitchen designers and orders began pouring in. Fred hurriedly turned to a California manufacturer, then one in Tennessee, but neither he nor his customers were satisfied.

Fred wasn't giving up. "I finally said, 'Shoot, somebody needs to do this,' " he recalls. " 'I'm gonna figure out a way to get this done. I think I could sell these.' It had the classic look and performance; the 12,000 to 15,000 BTU burners instead of 4,000. I finally said, 'We just need to do this ourselves.' "

Fred gathered a group of ten partners, including his doctor, the local Chevron distributor, an insurance agent, and several farmers, each of whom put in an average of about $12,000, and he rented an abandoned factory in town — plenty of those around with plants and jobs moving out.

He hired a couple of dozen local guys, none of them with any particular expertise. Did he just point to a bunch of stuff and say, "Make me a stove"? "Yup, sure did," Fred says. "That's about what it amounted to."

Fred had them disassemble a stove and put the parts they needed to buy on one side of the room and the parts they needed to make on the other side and they went from there. In 1989 he started building stoves.

Fred was advised to move his growing company to a bigger town, like Atlanta or at least Jackson, Mississippi. "I said, 'Well, I guess I'm going to have to put it in Jackson,' that's about as far as I was willing to go, to the capital about eighty-five miles from here. I figured I could recruit more people there and it would be more appropriate for a corporate headquarters to be in a bigger city, so I rented an office and drove down there."

But Fred's a local boy at heart. "I was a fish out of water in Jackson, the big city," he says. "And it just struck me one day: 'I don't

103

like this, it doesn't feel right.' So I gave up my office and said, 'I'm gonna do it in Greenwood or I'm not gonna do it at all.' "

Well, then, Fred, how about moving the plant to Mexico to save some bucks? No, Fred didn't want to do that either.

As the story goes Fred so far has built hundreds of thousands of these stainless steel behemoths right here in Greenwood, and sells them to the tune of roughly (Fred isn't telling) $300 million a year. And he's brought his hometown of Greenwood along for the ride.

Fred employs 1,300 local folks here in Greenwood, one of the most poverty-stricken areas of the country, which has lost thousands of jobs in recent years.

It's really almost more of a fairy tale than a folktale. Fred's *stove* became a status symbol, which is a lot like turning a pumpkin into a royal coach. Previously the stove had been at about the same prestige level as the water heater.

People were buying his stoves who didn't even cook on them. Fine with Fred. They were installing $50,000, even $100,000 "caterer's kitchens" with two dishwashers, wine coolers, refrigerators the size of meat lockers, and granite countertops big enough for F-15 landings — with Viking stoves as their focal points. Many of the same people were buying $75,000 all-terrain, four-wheel-drive Range Rovers, with rhino guards on the front, to drive to the mall and the Burger King drive-thru. Packing 15,000 BTUs per burner, Viking owners don't want to keep up with the Joneses, they wanted to *caramelize* them.

The Viking became a star of film and television, appearing whenever the set needed to say "upscale." But, really, a status symbol from Mississippi? A "trophy" kitchen appliance? Selling like hotcakes at $3,000 to $10,000 apiece? C'mon. I'd sooner believe the devil gives guitar lessons at midnight down at the intersection of 61 and 49.

The legend grows. Fred has swept in and become something of a one-man urban renewal project. He's purchased and is restoring at least thirteen buildings, a lot in a small town, most for Viking offices, some to rent to new businesses.

He's restored the 1903 opera house, overlooking the Yazoo River and sporting curlicue ironwork, and turned it into Viking's corporate headquarters. He remodeled the abandoned Ford dealer showroom, making it a tiered kitchen classroom for training dealers from around the world and holding Viking cooking-school classes.

So that dealers and visiting executives and cooking-school students would have a nice place to stay, Fred restored the abandoned dilapidated Irving Hotel, which dominated downtown and symbolized the state of things in Greenwood — and does once again.

Surprising as it is that Viking ranges are created in this small Mississippi town, it is just as surprising to find a world-class boutique luxury hotel here that many travel writers say is easily the finest in the state. "We have a premium product, an expensive product," Fred says of his stoves, "and it was difficult for us to find accommodations commensurate with our product line." So the old Irving received a $10 million makeover to become the new fifty-room Alluvian Hotel.

And it's not just dealers who stay there. There are lots of stove *groupies,* customers who so love their Vikings that they make pilgrimages to this mecca to take a Viking cooking class and tour the factory where their stove was born.

A van picks them up at the hotel for their tour of the plant where they see eighteen-gauge steel and parts turned into stoves in about three hours. Above the assembly line fly flags of the eighty countries where Viking sells stoves, ranging from a small apartment model to a six-burner monster with a griddle and a charcoal grill. They'll whip up a twelve-burner model if you want. Each stove is made to order, no inventory, with prices ranging from about $3,500 to $10,000.

Most of those on the tour are also taking a class or two at the Viking cooking school. Viking culinary arts centers are open in fourteen cities around the country teaching a nation how to cook now that they have the stoves.

Tonight's class is Gumbo 101, followed by Duck. The classes have a distinct local flavor, accompanied by a blues guitarist, and the instructor saying things like, "Any questions about the molasses-bourbon marinade or about what to do with the ducks once you've shot 'em?"

Most of the students in this class are middle-aged men, and they're either Viking owners or here for a test drive. "I'd love to own one," says one. "It's a manly stove. I don't want to cook on some girly-looking thing. My wife's trying to make me learn to cook so she doesn't have to."

They're staying at the hotel on a two-day cooking package.

"I have a Viking at home. A gas grill, six-burner," says Clifford, another student. "It looks good, and it makes you look like you know what you're doing. We have parties in our house and find that most people gather in the kitchen. It's become a centerpiece."

Others accuse him of bragging. There is a lot of stove envy. The men talk about the power of the beast. "We had an ice storm that knocked out the electricity for days," says one. "Heated our whole house with our Viking."

"I'm getting a six-burner with the griddle," says Phillip. "Whether or not you use it, it sounds great to say, 'Yeah, I've got the griddle in the middle.'"

Across from the luxury hotel, work proceeds on the Alluvian Spa . . . and the new artesian bakery. There's Viking's Delta Fresh Market & Deli, which is an organic market that sells gourmet food products with an upscale restaurant serving Southern dishes.

"One of our visitors said we were the new SoHo," remarks Carol Puckett Daily, who heads the new Viking Hospitality Group (hotel, restaurant, and cooking school), "and everybody from here went, 'What's SoHo?'"

Will all this fly in rural Mississippi? I try to imagine good ol' boys riding into town in their pickups for croissants and peppermint pedicures. "We're creating our own market," Carol says. "The hotel is 100 percent full tonight and that happens a lot of weekends, so it's working."

Why is his hometown so important to Fred? "This little town is like everyone's hometown," he says. "It's special to us. It's where we grew up, it's where our friends and relationships were formed, and it's a neat little place that through changes in the cotton industry and the economy has had some really difficult times and you hate to see that."

Fred seems bent on rejuvenating the entire Delta. The Alluvian offers Delta Discovery packages, such as the Delta Blues Tour with stops at clubs and historic sites, like the three separate grave sites of Robert Johnson, all claiming to be the real one. Other blues legends such as Muddy Waters, Mississippi John Hurt, B. B. King, and Son House are all from these parts. The Greenwood Blues Heritage Museum and Gallery is just down the street from Fred's hotel and he is on the advisory board of the B. B. King Museum that's under way over in Indianola. "Blues tourism!" he says. "It could save this old state."

There are Delta food tours, cotton tours (to include Cottonlandia and the still-functioning cotton exchange in Greenwood), literary tours, you name it. "Tennessee Williams is from right up the road," says Fred, on a roll now. "A lot of talent came out of this place, musical and literary. William Faulkner up in Oxford, Eudora Welty down in Jackson. We have a rich heritage in the fine arts. We're kind of an unappreciated state in some ways."

Maybe they should change the name of the town to Viking. Or better yet, how about Fred? Fred, Mississippi.

Would that every small town in America had a local boy at heart, like Fred.

THE ALIEN HIGHWAY

RACHEL, NEVADA, POP: 98

Rachel, Nevada: only place I ever had a gun drawn on me; only place I ever had breakfast with a space alien.

Two hours north of Las Vegas, out on Route 375 in no-man's-land, you come upon the desert town of Rachel, not much more than a small congregation of dusty trailers and other species of manufactured homes — and not even all that many of those, really. The sign heading into town doesn't even bother to mention population, just RACHEL . . . ELEV 4,970.

The road has been officially designated the Extraterrestrial Highway, the UFO Highway, or the Alien Highway, whichever you prefer, because there are more reported

UFO sightings and close encounters of the third kind here than anywhere else in the world. And also because the highway passes by the rather mysterious, semisecret, closed-to-the-public Groom Lake government test facility, aka Area 51. Featured in the film *Men in Black,* Area 51 is where the stealth bomber and other aircraft were rather stealthily developed, and where a disturbing number of our fellow Americans believe the government keeps alien spaceships as well as the aliens themselves, dead or alive.

Rachel is often referred to as the "UFO Capital," which would make the bar and grill (one of two detectable businesses in town) named the Little A'Le'Inn the Capitol and White House, with its proprietors, Pat and Joe Travis, the first family of UFOs.

Outside, a sign bearing the likeness of a typical alien — gray, inverted teardrop-shaped head, almond-eyed — reads EARTH-LINGS ALWAYS WELCOME, and inside there's WELCOME UFOS AND CREWS, which is cute, except: they're not exactly kid-ding.

Pat and Joe appear to be a salt-of-the-earth, fiftysomething couple. Joe looks like a cowboy, lean and tough, with a lined, sun-burned face that features a beard and mus-tache and usually a dangling cigarette. Pat wears no makeup and a short, practical haircut. They look like they might have come out here on a Conestoga wagon — one that broke down on its way to somewhere more hospitable to human life.

They say they're here because they felt a calling. "I somehow felt compelled," says Joe. "A lady from Arizona came in all upset because she'd been abducted a number of times. So Pat talked to her about it. Maybe that's why we're here, to help people, I don't know."

Theirs is a UFO ministry serving cold beer and Alien Burgers that Joe never fails to say are "out of this world." And the couple is here to offer a sympathetic ear to those who come to tell of their sightings and abductions.

"A man just came in and said he'd woken up in the middle of the night and found an alien in his living room," says Pat, with Joe adding enthusiastically, "Watching his TV!" Maybe that's all the space invaders want. Maybe they don't get cable in their area.

"These people are not out in left field," Pat states. "Some have been abducted, some more than once." Does she believe them? "Absolutely. One woman was chased by a UFO for fifty miles. They didn't abduct her because she was over her childbearing years." Whew. I'm good to go.

"We've been encountered ourselves," she continues. "Psychics counted twenty-seven alien beings in here one night." Which is not good. They take all the tables and don't spend a dime.

"We've had signs that our mission is not complete," Pat says: pulsating lights, even with the circuit breaker off, when the two were discussing moving from Rachel. "We make a decent living," Joe says, "which is all we can hope for until we're released."

In addition to a bar and restaurant, the Little A'Le'Inn is actually an inn, a motel of sorts, consisting of four or five mobile homes, each divided into two guest rooms. We meet some interesting folks you probably would not at the Ritz. Ladell, a waitress in the restaurant, tells me of the night she woke up to see "a big blue glowing ball drifting around my living room. I tried to lift my head but could not. The next morning I had a strange circle mark on my thigh. When people come in here now and say they saw strange beams of light, I believe 'em."

The restaurant is small, so you sometimes double up at a table with someone you don't know. A stranger. One morning I join a man dressed all in black and topped with a black hat. To be friendly-like, I strike up a conversation, introducing myself as Bill from New York, and asking where he hails from. "I am Ambassador Merlin from the Alpha Dracona star system in this galaxy," he replies. I'm caught off guard and say, "So . . . how was your flight in?"

Over humanoid food (apparently they eat two eggs up with bacon and toast for breakfast in his star system, too) the Ambassador says there are definitely live alien beings at Area 51, but not to worry, they're here to help us advance so that we can join the United Federation of Planets. That sounds good. Will there be dues?

Just down the street is the Area 51 Research Center, operated by Glen not-the-singer Campbell, whose goal is to find out what's really going on over the ridge in Area 51, aka Dreamland. He's not interested so much in alleged sightings and abductions, he wants to see hardware, spaceships. Campbell also has an apartment in Las Vegas across the street from the airport, where he observes the comings and goings of allegedly unscheduled aircraft ferrying government employees commuting to and from Area 51.

"It's interesting here in Rachel," Glen says. "I've met a Venutian, a Pleiades woman, and beings from all over the galaxy. This is a place that brings out the extremes in people.

A light in the sky is like a Rorschach test. Some see UFOs, some see aircraft, some see God himself." There are definitely unidentified flying objects in the Nevada skies, but what? Glen thinks they're experimental aircraft.

At dusk, visitors trek out of town to a sacred site for true believers, the Black Mailbox (since stolen and replaced by a white one), a veritable bus stop for UFOs. Chuck Clark leads small tours to the mailbox, explaining this night to three engineering students and a couple from Texas some of the amazing things that have been seen here.

"I've seen a craft streak thousands of miles an hour across the sky and stop on a dime," he says. "The aliens at Area 51 are probably not hostile, they're probably cooperating with our government to help us develop aircraft like their own."

"I feel love toward them," says Charlene Finkner from Lubbock of the aliens from outer space, "although I wouldn't want them performing experiments on me."

"We have no reason to disbelieve they exist," Chuck concludes, but then no one in Rachel does.

Back at the Little A'Le'Inn, I check out the extensive souvenir selection — T-shirts, caps, patches, lighters, books — and a rack filled with all manner of UFO magazines and books, like *The UFO Etiquette and Survival Handbook,* for the potential abductee. There are also videos, such as the $40 *Visitors from Space,* touting itself as the first-place winner in the Abductee-Contactee category at the UFO Film Festival of 1993. In Cannes. Or maybe Pluto?

There is also an alarming assortment of what might delicately be called wacko conspiracy periodicals, with articles on such subjects as the New World Order (think the United Nations run by Secretary-General Darth Vader) readying to take over the globe via fleets of black helicopters, described as "helicopter life forms." Another good reason why we Americans must all keep our guns.

Alas, Joe espouses such beliefs. Standing behind the bar one evening, he explains to me that members of the eastern-liberal-media establishment, like myself, along with the Washington politicians haven't a clue what's going on with the underground conspiracy to take over our country and the world. Why, we probably haven't noticed the codes imprinted on the back of every stop sign to direct NWO tanks; we don't know that the owners of the world's largest banks and higher-ups in the government, the military, and the media are part of the conspiracy. He goes on like this for two hours and six beers apiece. (I like a bartender who matches his customers drink for drink; only then can he honestly determine when it's time to cut them off.)

Joe, popping his seventh beer and sliding another to me, is getting worked up. "You're too stupid to realize that the Rhodes Scholar program is a training ground for leaders of the New World Order!"

"What?" I reply. And when he re-shouts his statement I retort, slowly and emphatically, "You . . . are a complete . . . f — — ing . . . idiot!"

To which Joe responds by reaching beneath the bar and pulling a gun on me. A six-shooter if I recall correctly. Which, I have to say, did win me over to his way of thinking.

BOMBSVILLE

MCALESTER, OKLAHOMA, POP: 17,783

In McAlester, Oklahoma, it's one of those heavenly spring Sunday mornings. Outside the Baptist church dogwoods and rosebuds blossom in the warm sunshine.

Inside, the organist is playing "Onward Christian Soldiers," a hymn I must have sung a hundred times when I was a child. I liked it. It was familiar and easy to sing, so everybody joined in, their voices filling the church, and rousing us from the sermon's drone.

To me, its message was to be strong in our faith, strong enough to live by the Golden Rule despite daily temptations to do otherwise, no matter what. But this day, in McAlester in the days following America's invasion of Iraq, I'm hearing the hymn in a different way:

Onward Christian soldiers, marching as to war;
With the cross of Jesus, going on before.

Reverend Terry Moore's sermon this day is about finding just and righteous cause in the Bible for the new war in Iraq. "Ecclesiastes 3:8 says there is a time for war and a time for peace," says Reverend Moore. "You turn through the Bible and you won't ever find a passage that condemns war. God hates war, but sometimes God uses war as a way to achieve His objectives, ridding a dictator or sin in a nation."

Reverend Moore, a bespectacled man in his thirties, is not really preaching. He speaks rather softly and in a matter-of-fact way to his small congregation of seemingly simple folk, who have arrived in modest cars and unassuming attire. Many of the men are showing their colors: an American flag tie, an American flag on the back of a jacket, several American flag lapel pins. The reverend wears a suit and tie, unadorned by robes.

"As we go to John 3:16," he continues, "we're gonna see what God has to say about war. He says we have the right to protect ourselves. And the Constitution guarantees us the right to bear arms. And he who has no sword let him sell his garment and buy one to protect our families and freedoms.

"We've already lost servicemen in Iraq," says Reverend Moore. "To me they're heroes, the men that sacrificed these freedoms, the freedom to go to Wal-Mart or go fishing."

The congregation sings *"Glory, glory, hallelujah! His truth is marching on,"* as the collection plate is passed.

They conclude the religious service with "The Star-Spangled Banner," and church and state are neatly, simply one.

The next time I see the reverend he is driving a forklift at the bomb factory. You wouldn't know it by looking, but the peaceful little town of McAlester makes virtually all of America's bombs, and has since the factory opened in 1943. There's no "Welcome to Bombsville" sign when you drive into town (only a perplexing one that reads HOME OF COWBOYS AND ITALIANS). The high-school teams aren't "The Bombardiers."

Yet it's no secret where the plant is or what it produces: everything from 20 mm tank shells to the 5,000-pound bunker busters. It was built way out here in the middle of the country in 1943 so that German and Japanese planes couldn't reach it. The plant has since produced all of the (nonnuclear) bombs dropped on Germany, Japan, Korea, Vietnam, Serbia, Kuwait, Afghanistan, and, now, Iraq. Not to mention sales to foreign nations.

Mayor Dale Covington watches the war on TV with special pride. "Of course, I see an explosion and think, 'There goes another McAlester bomb.' We're proud of it, proud of our workers. They take a lot of pride in the way they build bombs."

"Shock and awe" in Baghdad means more jobs and overtime in McAlester, where the bomb factory has tripled the number of workers on the production line and started its first night shift since Vietnam. Bombs are McAlester's business, and business is booming.

"We're still hiring," says Colonel Jyuji Hewitt, commanding officer of the McAlester Army Ammunition Plant. "We are the largest employer in this area and if you look at number two and three it's the state prison [where an execution was scheduled that night] and Wal-Mart [which is gutting the quaint downtown]." For the plant's 1,200 civilian employees, pay starts at $15 an hour plus benefits — a figure the prison and Wal-Mart can't match.

It's Colonel Hewitt's task to keep up with demand. (Production reportedly went way up more than a year before the war began.) So, the colonel looks at the war a little differently than anybody else.

"Sometimes I see bombs being dropped on TV," he says, "and I say, 'Boy, that's several days' work right there.'" But he is proud. "Sometimes I see a bomb exploding and say, 'Yeah, that's a McAlester calling card right there.'"

Out here, folks still make bombs the old-fashioned way, by hand, in the 500-pound variety, the 2,000-pounder, and the super-sized 5,000-pound bunker buster. And while the colonel won't confirm it, they almost certainly built the new 21,000-pound MOAB (Mother of All Bombs) here too.

On the outside, the ramshackle factory buildings appear to be the original hastily constructed structures, lightly maintained. Inside one building, workers in static-free jumpsuits mix a large kettle of warm, wet, gooey, gray plastic bonded explosives, a lethal witches' brew. In another they're filling the bomb casings like so many pastry chefs.

Indeed, Loretta Russell is a grandmother

who looks like she really ought to be home baking pies instead of here examining eight-foot-tall bombs dangling from chains that extend from an overhead conveyor belt.

"I don't guess I'm real proud of the fact I make bombs and what they're used for," she says. "But it's necessary and has to be done to help support our country. I feel like they (Iraqis) asked for it; they kind of started this."

Morale at the plant is high. "With the war on, it's going through the roof," says Aaron Kilburne, a third-generation bomb worker. The workers are making money and it gives them a sense of purpose. "I wish there wasn't such a thing as war," he says, "but if there's a war I want to win."

Billy Joe Pink faced a hiring freeze due to budget cuts in his chosen field, teaching, so he turned to bomb-making, where there are jobs. "The bomb business is good business," Billy Joe says.

To many it's just a job. To others it's a source of patriotic pride. Many do reflect on what they're doing. "I'm not dropping 'em, but I'm making 'em," says Luke Tucker, "and I think, 'Well, am I hurting innocent people or anything?' " Would he rather be working in a candy factory? "Yes I would," he says, "if it paid as much."

"When I see something explode over there," says Loretta, now up on a riser placing fuses into the bombs, "I think, 'Did my hands help make that?' I'd rather help Santa make toys, that's what I'd really like to do."

Aaron points out that this is a far cry from working in a candy factory: "This stuff can kill ya'. " Indeed, there's a monument here to twenty-five workers who've lost their lives at the plant. One name on the memorial is Clarence C. Moore, Reverend Moore's grandfather.

I ask the reverend if he thinks that making bombs while being a messenger for the Prince of Peace — "Do unto others," "Turn the other cheek," "Love thine enemy" — is at all contradictory.

"No," he says, "as I read the Bible and pray about it, there's some times you have to do things necessary to protect our freedoms, and building bombs, that's one of the things."

Does what he's doing out here, making bombs that blow people to kingdom come, ever give him pause? "Not really," he answers. "I wish we didn't have these jobs, wish we didn't have this plant. That would be the ultimate, that we don't have to make bombs anymore, that we don't have to have a military. But that would be utopia. Reality sets in." With Reverend Moore it's "praise the Lord and pass the ammunition."

Bombs are shipped out continuously from the plant by truckload and trainload. Others are stored in igloo bunkers that dot the rolling, wooded hills of this vast 45,000-acre tract like giant mushrooms. Tens of thousands of the deadly devices lie peacefully cohabitating with the woodpeckers, wild turkeys, deer, coyotes, and bobcats. "We have hunting, camping, fishing, and boating here," says Bill Starry, the natural resources manager for the bomb factory. There are one hundred lakes here and a small stream, which you cross as you're leaving the bomb factory grounds, marked "Peaceable Creek."

ILLEGAL PORCH FURNITURE

WILSON, NORTH CAROLINA,
POP: 44,405

This is the city: Wilson, North Carolina, a pleasant, peaceful little town of tobacco auctions, antique shops, and good barbecue. In springtime folks still blossom on their front porches like flowers on the dogwoods and magnolia.

But this spring is different. Wilson is in the grip of a crime wave. Many of the town's seemingly upstanding citizens are sitting down . . . sitting down on . . . Illegal Porch Furniture!

The story you are about to read is true: Wilson has passed a law banning old, dilapidated, upholstered indoor furniture from outdoor porches, not because it's unsafe — in some cases the offending piece of furniture is a car seat with safety belts — but really just because town officials seem to think it's . . . tacky.

Tacky, illegal? In America? Since when? If that were true, wouldn't lawn-ornament stores be shut down? Thomas Kinkade art shops raided by SWAT teams? Wouldn't air strikes be called in on the whole of Las Vegas?

Prime offenders in Wilson are synthetic leather ("pleather") covered chairs — frequently recliners — and overstuffed sofas. Unfortunately, they're not usually relegated to the porch until worn and no longer fit for the living room. Finer garden shops tend not to sell red pleather recliner chairs. And once outdoors, indoor furniture is defenseless against the elements. Criminal couches were not born bad, they're victims of their environments.

9:00 a.m. We head over to city hall to ask Mayor C. Bruce Rose about the new law. He himself seems presentable enough: clean-shaven with hair neatly combed, dressed in a white shirt, nicely pressed double-breasted suit, and shined shoes. We don't care for his tie, but he'd be a credit to any porch.

"It's to beautify the city," the mayor says, by way of explaining the new ordinance. "We're dealing with junk on porches. Absolute junk. That's what this is all about."

10:00 a.m. We next question one Queen (her name, not title) Barnes, a member of the Wilson Appearance Commission, which drafted the law. Her home is beyond reproach. She has tasteful, tidy landscaping with nicely pruned bushes and no porch furniture at all, leaving no room for criticism. She herself is handsomely dressed. She could be Martha Stewart, except she's black, lives in Wilson not Bedford Hills, and isn't an ex-con. No sign of an electronic ankle bracelet monitor.

"The Wilson Appearance Commission is dedicated to assuring the aesthetic values of the community," she says, and referring to illicit porch furniture: "These unpleasantries should not be there."

11:00 a.m. We take a statement from Vera Pope, a gray-haired lady who started the porch-furniture movement, and has been known to rat out her neighbors. She's planting flowers in front of her well-kept home when we roll up. She agrees to take us on a walking tour.

"Now this is an eyesore," she says, pointing to a large tattered couch on a front porch. It is a modern, beige, curved-back, armless model with sunburst pleats — the look one might encounter in, say, the pop-out family room of a late-model RV or manufactured home. (What chance did it ever have?) "That needs to go," Ms. Pope concludes.

She pronounces the same verdict on a black pleather recliner chair with a split seat on a neighbor's porch. It's definitely not a part of the Ralph Lauren French Country Garden Collection and appears to be a clear violation of Section 3.3 of the Community Appearance Standards: ". . . a visual blight and detriment, inhibits property values, deters tourism and otherwise discourages the comfort, happiness and emotional stability of all citizens."

One might fairly ask: What tourism? And secondly: Might not it be the law itself that's discouraging the comfort, happiness, and emotional stability of Wilson's citizenry?

Noon. We conduct a series of man-on-the-porch interviews. "I think it's a bunch of foolishness, myself," says an elderly man lying on a porch swing that, by definition, is clearly in compliance.

"I don't see why the city has the right to tell me that I can't have a couch on my porch," says another. "It's not bothering anybody. It's not a menace to society."

"I don't understand," says an enormous woman, who proclaims that she's sitting in her favorite chair. "Why should we have to get rid of something that's comfortable to us, as long as it looks decent?" (We were unable to make visual contact with any part of the chair to evaluate its decency or lack thereof.)

"It seems like law enforcement would have better things to do," says another man. "I have a friend who's buying an old couch for his porch just to see what happens." Seeds of insurgency.

"I believe a man has the right to have a couch on his porch," yet another man pronounces. "I will take them to the Supreme Court and fight for my rights." (Porch furniture is not specifically mentioned in the Bill of Rights, nor under either the shalts or shalt nots in the Ten Commandments.)

1 p.m. We go out on a reconnaissance sweep of potential problem areas. We knock on some doors to ask people about their porch furniture. We can hear them inside, but no one answers. In these uncertain times, people apparently do not want to talk to The Man about their porch furniture without an attorney present.

During recon we stumble upon a big drug bust going down right before our eyes at one of the houses. Wow! What luck! A TV correspondent and his crew happen upon an exclusive, action-packed story. We go for coffee and wait for the hard news to blow over.

2:30 p.m. We pay a visit to Councilman Bob Braxton, who voted against the ban and favors decriminalizing illegal porch furniture. His porch furniture is highly tasteful: *real wicker.* He says it holds up well because it's on a covered porch. Mine just went to hell outside, so I was wondering.

"I know that a lot of these old chairs and couches don't look good," he says, "but I'm sure there're a lot of people that sit on 'em that are at ease with the world."

And just as with other crime categories, such as manslaughter and armed robbery, there is an economic component to the crime. The burden falls most heavily on the poor. Drive through the campuses of our finest colleges and universities and you will see broke students who are otherwise law-abiding, more or less, sitting on unsightly porch furniture. Sorry, they don't have the disposable income or the inclination to invest in a Brown Jordan teak patio set, which by the way isn't half as comfortable. For hours of outdoor leisurely porch-sitting, nothing beats the comfort of a well-worn Barcalounger or La-Z-Boy.

The new law has everybody riled up. We're told that one melodramatic Southern newspaper columnist likened the brouhaha to

General Sherman's burning of Atlanta! Another writer said that getting rid of porch furniture was going to destroy the oral tradition of the South resulting in no more William Faulkners! I was unaware that Faulkner wrote while sitting on his porch in a raggedy pleather La-Z-Boy. But there is certainly the tradition of sitting on the front porch, enjoying the air, talking to companions and to neighbors walking by. It's called "visiting." There are innumerable threats to this tradition: in most neighborhoods people don't walk anymore, and if and when they do they're wearing Walkmans so you can't talk to them anyway. Yet another Southern writer called the porch-furniture ban "the ultimate yuppification of the South." The New South, where nice people don't sit on the front porch (look for 'em out back on the patio), where they don't keep a rusty car up on blocks in the yard . . . and where each community will have to wrestle with the question: Is rigid gentrification better than tastelessness?

"I don't think it has anything to do with Southern tradition," says Mayor Rose. "I really don't. It is an appearance ordinance that deals with the beauty of the city, that deals with junk."

3:15 p.m. We ride along on porch-furniture

133

patrol with city inspector Jeff Winstead in his immaculate patrol car. He could eat off his floor mats. I do. Fries usually, that I've fumbled at the drive-thru. His personal appearance was beyond reproach: trim, well dressed, with an obvious knack for personal hygiene.

At our first stop, he inspects a porch glider with peeling paint. It's a classic metal one, circa probably the 1940s, that would fetch a fortune in some trendy antique shop.

"This is actually serviceable," he says, giving it a swing. Apparently he just wants to make sure it's not hopelessly broken-down junk.

4:00 p.m. Inspector Winstead gets a tip on a possible UPFS — unauthorized porch furniture situation — in progress. Jeff has a keen eye. Spots it half a block away. It's orange. Plush. Modern. A stunner that does certainly brighten up the drab neighborhood. Winstead stays cool, exiting the vehicle and walking calmly to the chair, inspecting all the way. "The arms and seat are a bit worn," he notes. Does the color bother him? "The color doesn't bother me at all," he answers. *It doesn't?* Has the inspector had any special training for this position? Has the town sent him to the Academy of Used-and-Not-All-That-Good-in-the-First-Place Furniture Evaluation?

We are so distracted by the big orange blob that we fail to notice a positively felonious chair on the other side of the porch: black pleather severely cracked on the arms, exposing lots of beige foam padding.

Now this one must be in violation. "Yes, it is," says Officer Winstead. "The matting underneath is ripped and torn and falling down too. This one is a definite candidate for removal."

Candidate for removal. I mean they can't just bust onto the porch and start carting away a man's porch furniture. This is still America, isn't it?

"So you'll write 'em up?" I ask.

He pulls out a book of tickets that reads: "During a recent inspection of this property the following appearance concerns or problems were noticed." He checks the box for "Worn Out, Deteriorated or Abandoned Household or Office Furniture."

I wanted to grab a bullhorn and announce: "Come out with your hands up!" Always wanted to do that. Instead, I read the chair its Veranda rights: "You have the right to (continue to) remain silent. You have the right to a hearing with an attorney present. You have the right to be upholstered . . ."

"There seem to be some gray areas," I say.

"You're gonna have to make some judgment calls."

"Definitely," he answers. "A hearing officer would make the final determination."

A hearing officer? There would actually be a hearing held on the rights of this chair to remain free? That's more than we give some humans these days.

Would the chair be present? "Probably not," says the inspector. "Probably just photos." Crime scene photos! Do easy chairs have DNA? Would an attorney be hired to represent the chair? Would the hearing be held by a decorator?

"We would be authorized to issue a series of escalating fines," the inspector explains, "$25 for the first day, $50 for the second day, and $100 a day for each day thereafter that the violation continues to exist."

We cruise by a porch furnished with an old mattress and another with an old refrigerator; neither in the gray area. But at the other end of the spectrum, we spot a like-new L-shaped sectional couch, white, with eight neatly arranged matching throw pillows, sitting out on a lawn *in front* of the porch. Looks like a setup. We keep rolling, and see two pleather office chairs with wheels, two blue-gray bucket car seats, a lavender plush chair, and a plaid couch in brown tones.

In Wilson, North Carolina, illegal porch furniture is on the run. Perpetrators are still on the loose, on the porches, but not for long. The lucky ones will be placed in re-upholstery programs. The others will face stiff fines and possible life sentences at the city sanitation facility.

Arriving late at the motel, as is my custom, I often get the last room in the inn: smoking, handicapped, next to the (ding . . . ding . . . ding) elevator,

Trail's end at the Wigwam Motel

and the (thunk-thunk-Thunk) ice machine, over the lounge, open 'til 2:00 a.m., and, lucky me, it's karaoke night! The room faces east, nearest the expressway, and the curtains don't quite close, so a laser beam of sunlight awakens me at dawn if the eighteen-

Artist Duffy Lyon with her Butter Cow masterpiece

wheelers don't get to me first. If you spend enough time on the road, this may all happen to you in a single night. Of course you've gotta have a little luck.

Pat and Joe at the Little A'L'Inn

Some of our TV crews live on the road, staying with the same hotel chain whenever possible, thereby

"Viva Las Vegas," as sung in an RV on the Strip with the King

racking up millions of points and free vacations on Mars. One crew I've worked with are faithful Marriotteers, at times spending thirty nights or more straight at one when covering an important ongoing story, like this month's Trial, or Storm, of the Century. One year they stayed more than three hundred nights at Marriotts. If there wasn't a Marriott where we were working, they were glad to drive back and forth to the nearest one a hundred miles away.

These guys were way beyond the platinum level. More like Elite Triple-Black, Diamond-Encrusted, Electroplated Golden Toe Ring Club. They probably hold secret club meetings.

So when we check in, I am sent to my modest roomette, while they're sticking their keys into the special slot on the elevator that gives them access to the Concierge Level, where they are lavished with swank accommodations, moisturizing soaps and beautifying emollients, minibars containing fine wines and whole cashews and $9 Snickers bars, complimentary bottled water, Internet access, newspapers, hors d'oeuvres, and three-egg omelets. At their level, they can probably stay in the general manager's home and sleep with his wife.

My Axiom of Business Travel: The number of nights spent in a hotel or motel is inversely proportional to the quality of that hotel or motel. (Corollary: The amount of time spent in a town is inversely proportional to the desire to be there.)

For example, when we check into, say, the world-renowned Frontenac Hotel in Quebec, or the swank Gaylord Texan in Grapevine, Texas, in the midnight hour and the desk clerk is telling us about the four-star restaurants, the designer golf course, spa, and boutique shoppes, we'll be staying there for six or seven hours. I always ask if we can go ahead and check out while we're checking in if we promise not to steal the bathrobes. Having grown unaccustomed to amenities at cheap motels, I once awakened at a nice hotel with a chocolate mint stuck to the side of my head.

But when we check into the Beaver Motel in Beaver, Oklahoma (a bit overpriced, I thought, at $37.50) — a mid-century concrete-block motor lodge featuring extension cords running all over my room (floor, ceiling, and eye level), no towel racks, a toilet that doesn't exactly flush, a phone line dangling from the ceiling, a little trash left beside the bed from the last guest, a large hole in the wall patched with bare drywall, and carpeting that made me vow never to remove my shoes again — it's for three nights. Actually I left after two, driving three hours through a dust storm to Amarillo,

Texas, to get out of there on "urgent business."

The Beaver o'er-leaped the Relax Motel in Folkston, Georgia, on my list of unassuming accommodations. The Relax, or "Reflux" as we called it, is the kind of place that makes you dream of a Motel 6. In fact, I spotted one our first day there but it was a mirage. Three nights. These small, old motels throughout the country all seem to be owned by Indians (the from-India kind), in much the same peculiar way that nail salons are owned by Koreans and umbrella salesmen on the streets in New York are all from Senegal. Odd.

A wary Indian couple checked me in. They stood behind bulletproof glass with a little hole for passing them credit cards and driver's licenses. The guest checking in stands outside in the parking lot.

The door to my room was heavy-gauge steel, and when it slammed behind me, the thought occurred to me that I might not be able to check out without appearing before a parole board. There were holes in the wall where amenities such as the towel racks had been removed. The pillows were the exact opposite of downy, the carpet crusty.

The most striking proof of my axiom came in Nevada, where I was somehow given an upgrade at the fabulous Egyptian-themed, pyramid-shaped Luxor Hotel on the Vegas strip, from the economy slave's quarters to a King Tut suite at the top of the pyramid, with a living room, dining room, bar, guest room, and so many light switches I had to start making my rounds fifteen minutes before bedtime. We stayed there for about seven hours total, checking out early and driving a couple of hours north to the tiny desert town of Rachel, Nevada, where the motel consisted of four or five mobile homes, each divided into two guest rooms. There we stayed three long nights.

We rarely complain. But in Minneapolis on our way to Hayward, Wisconsin, we rented a car with some annoying buzz we couldn't locate and decided just to live with it. In the elevator at the Airport Hilton I heard a buzzing sound again, a sound that I could still hear in my room, which was next to the elevator. I decided it was some sort of electrical problem with the elevator, so I rolled my suitcase onto the buzzing elevator and went down to the front desk. They gave me a new room and said they'd get right on the problem. But the buzzing continued in the hallway and in the room. I figured it must be something in the hotel's whole electrical system. Or maybe in my head! Was I going mad? I opened my suitcase and the buzzing became louder; louder still when I opened my Dopp Kit and found my electric toothbrush had kicked on.

I've been fortunate. I've stayed at a Holiday Inn in Indiana that provided guests with complimentary flyswatters and books of matches with our names imprinted on them. After lobbying for two days at the front desk, I was named "Guest of the Day" at the Inn at St. Mary's in South Bend. This was announced on the in-house TV channel and I was given full use of the GOTD's special parking spot just steps from the entrance.

I've stayed at some unique inns: Wigwam Village in Cave City, Kentucky, where rooms are individual tepees, albeit made from concrete rather than buffalo hides, so perhaps they were erected in recent times. And the Quebec City hotel made completely of ice: sat on an ice seat in an ice booth in the ice bar drinking ice-cold vodka from an ice glass, then walked through the ice lobby to my ice room and slept on an ice bed. The hotel gets bigger every year, guests paying hundreds of dollars a night to experience this clear violation of the Geneva conventions. In Japan, I stayed in something called a capsule hotel, where the "rooms" look like coffins stacked in a hallway and are equipped with tiny TVs, phones, and side curtains.

And I've stayed at Caesars Pocono Resort

for romantic getaways, in a room with a seven-foot-tall champagne glass for couples' water sports. But, you know, it loses something when you're in there with two guys holding a camera and sound equipment.

Bad-Motel Warning Signs

1. Day rates . . . Hourly rates . . . Nominal charge for having sex in the parking lot
2. Sign boasts AIR-CONDITIONED! COLOR TV! PHONE!
3. "Vacancy" permanently painted on sign
4. Desk clerk speaks to you through small hole in bulletproof glass . . . while you stand outside
5. Reasonable room rates: $29.95 versus $109 at Budget Inn across the street
6. AAA plaque dated 1971
7. Sign in parking lot reads NOT RESPONSIBLE FOR GUNSHOT WOUNDS
8. Rabbit ears on RCA TV
9. Shell No-Pest Strips need changing
10. Picture of spotted owl with message: TO SAVE THE PLANET — WE RARELY WASH OUR SHEETS AND TOWELS
11. Towels like gauze bandages from first-aid kits
12. Sign reads: PLEASE LEAVE PLASTIC CUP FOR NEXT GUEST
13. The bed is hard . . .

14. . . . so's the bedspread
15. Shag carpeting a little crunchy
16. Half-eaten burrito under bed
17. Card reads: WELCOME, YOUR ROOM WAS CLEANED BY <u>BUSTER</u>
18. Minibar stocked with air freshener, bed-bug spray, and Mace
19. SAVE EVEN MORE. ASK ABOUT OUR STA-FRIENDLY SHARE-A-ROOM PLAN!
20. On room phone dial pad: PRESS #1 FOR POLICE, #2 FOR AMBULANCE, #3 FOR BAIL BONDS

THE COW PHOTOGRAPHER

NEW GLARUS, WISCONSIN, POP: 2,111

"Head up . . . Right foot forward . . . Turn . . . Work it . . ."

Kathy DeBruin looks into her Hasselblad camera and calls out a steady stream of fashion-photographer chatter.

"Now we're coming . . . Head up more . . . Now go away . . . Go away hard!"

This isn't easy. The model, Maggie, is plus-size and unclothed and Kathy is trying to make her look slim and angular, while showing off her attractive, umm, mammary glands. Readers of the publication where these pictures will appear like to see those. Maggie has nice legs, but not great legs. They could use a little, you know . . . *spray paint*. Kathy shakes a can of white flat enamel and touches up Maggie's gams. She paints slightly outside the lines, getting some white on the black areas, so she reaches into her large makeup case, takes out a can of WD-40 all-purpose aerosol liquid oil lubricant and protectant, sprays the errant white, and wipes it away.

If anyone can make Maggie look good, it's Kathy, what with Maggie being a Holstein cow and Kathy a cow photographer par excellence, the Annie Leibovitz of cow portraiture. Yes, a cow photographer, an occupation that probably doesn't exist where you live but seems not at all unusual to residents of this cheese-based culture.

This is Wisconsin, America's Dairyland, where the words "lactose" and "intolerant" are never to appear in the same publication. (After all, that digestive dysfunction is "just a theory" here in the "Dairy State.") And "Parkay" is a slur that could get you busted by the Wisconsin Hate Crimes Unit.

Kathy lives in the heart of dairyland, on a farm outside New Glarus, a well-châteaued town of cheese curds and cheese fondue, sincere yodelers and unapologetic accordionists, *Geschnetzeltes* and *Rahmschnitzel.* It's home to the Spotted Cow Ale brewery and the annual Heidi Festival. There's a monument downtown inscribed IN MEMORY OF

THE FIRST SETTLERS OF THE SWISS COLONY NEW GLARUS, and the town calls itself Little Switzerland.

Kathy's been a cow photographer for more than thirty years. She owns Agri-Graphics, a firm in New Glarus that employs photo-lab technicians and six photographers who travel the nation and the world taking cow pictures. The office has a U.S. Cow Density Map on the wall.

"Cows are what we're best at," Kathy says, noting that they also do occasional portraits of beef cattle, horses, sheep, pigs, dogs, cats — even a few humans. And not all of their cow portraits are for catalogs. Here in Wisconsin people love their cows. They're part of the family. Kathy shows me an engagement photo of a couple with cow (*per bovis*), a formal photograph of a wedding party in full regalia *p.b.,* a baby *p.b.,* family portraits *p.b.,* Christmas cards, business cards, and scenic cow photography. No bovine boudoir photography, I was pleased to note.

On a cool mid-April morning, Kathy dons a ski jacket and loads her green Chevy Blazer with a puzzling array of photographic equipment, baby powder, spray paint, potting soil, WD-40, camouflage netting, a shovel, and a goat. Kermit the goat. (Should someone call

Homeland Security?)

It's a sunny day, with birds singing, cows lowing, and a stainless steel milk truck backing up to her cow barn. She heads out of her long driveway, leaving behind her cows, horses, and dogs, then drives along a two-lane road past rolling fields, silos, barns, stands of trees, and (of course) more cows. It's a beautiful landscape, perhaps like Switzerland except no nagging Alps.

Kathy says she grew up on a farm but figured she'd get away from that way of life when she majored in art and zoology in college. "But the more I saw of the world," she says, "the more I thought the farm wasn't such a bad place." There isn't a crying need nor many entry-level jobs in cow photography. But she found a cow photographer who trained her on the job and she's been doing it ever since.

"When I began, a female coming onto the farm and telling these farmers what to do, it wasn't accepted very well," says Kathy, forty-four. "They'd do things the way they wanted and when they saw it didn't work so well, they gradually began listening to me."

Kathy pulls into a driveway and up to a barn where she greets the Stilling brothers: "Morning, Pete. Morning, Bud." They stroll into the barn, where Kathy meets some of today's subjects: Maggie, Angel, Lilly, Lillian, Molly — all being groomed and pampered and generally given tender loving care as the Young Rascals belt out "Good Lovin' " on the radio: *"Good Lovin'! All I need is love. Good Lovin'!"* The cows not having their portraits taken today are milked as the Rascals continue: *"Honey please squeeze me tight, don't you want your baby to be allright?"*

"They like pampering," Bud remarks, pushing up the bill of his University of Wisconsin Hockey cap. "Their milk production goes up the day they have their pictures taken." He offers me a sip of fresh milk straight from the udder, which of course I must accept, despite being so close to the source and in an aromatic barn atmosphere. It is still warm, creamy, and tasty. I've never really taken a liking to fat-free milk, which tastes like it came out of a garden hose.

The cows have been washed (twice) and are now being detailed (not de-tailed): brushed, clipped, and combed — much as your mother or teacher did to you on picture day at school. Except cows don't go to school and can't order wallet-size photographs to trade with their friends. Cows don't carry wallets. They're opposed to leather goods of any kind. Cows are basically vegans.

Their photographs will be published in glossy cow-sales catalogs and breeder's guides, which dairy farmers gape at like pimply teenage boys ogle *Playboy* and baby boomers swoon over Better (Than Anyone Else's) Kitchens & Bath magazines.

"A good picture will raise the sale price 10 to 20 percent or more," says Bud of these cows, which he hopes to sell for $2,500 to $3,500 apiece. "You've gotta get a picture that, when someone's leafing through the catalog they'll stop and say, 'Whoa! Look at that!' " Kathy DeBruin can do that. Her cow photographs are signed, like Picassos. She'll shoot these cows in a bucolic pasture that looks a lot like my screen saver. Bud has mowed for the occasion and removed a post that would have been in view of the camera.

"If I had my choice," Kathy says, "we'd eliminate the fence there. You want to avoid any lines that would create optical illusions and make the cow look less straight."

Bud leads Maggie out of the barn. She is docile, almost bovine you might say. At 1,500 pounds or so that's good. Kathy has a black-and-blue foot from a previous photo session. For a cow, Maggie looks pretty good. She's un-milked. Whereas some female runway models are completely flat-chested, dairy cows need ample, full udders to be attractive.

"We want some bloom in her udder," Bud says.

"She really does have a pretty little udder," Kathy comments. Nice compliment. "Might need a little pancake (makeup)."

"That bloom, straight back, smooth-skinned, clean-haired," Bud explains, "all mean she's healthy and gives more milk. You want to see that *dairy* character."

The ultimate compliment you can pay any cow is to say she looks "dairy." Kathy's goal here is to make each cow appear as "dairy" as possible. Having a full udder is certainly "dairy," but there are many other factors that go into that elusive quality of dairiness.

"We want them to look a bit taller in the front," Kathy says, and so she has them put their two front feet on a three-inch board, concealing it with silage. She places small drink-coaster-size squares under each foot because some buyers like to see the cow's toes. (Bovine hoof fetish! Next *Jerry Springer*!)

"We want their top lines straight," Kathy explains, meaning their backs. "Cows need straight backs with no sway at all to look their best." She spends most of her time on this feature. All the gals — Maggie, Angel, Lillian, and the others — sag a bit. We all do.

Humans have elective surgery, Kathy is into cosmetology. Heavily. She's a cow stylist, using everything but lipstick in the conduct of her extreme makeovers. No aging movie star ever received such refurbishing.

"Tail back . . . Rear foot back . . . Ears forward . . . Teat back . . ." (You can say "teat" on the farm? Cool.)

Angel is next and needs a little powder. A lot of powder actually. In fact, spray paint. Kathy touches up a couple of leg spots with white paint and brushes talcum powder into her white hide. She piles an inch or two of the powder onto indentations on Angel's back, sculpting it with a spatula to make a straight line. Next she teases some of Angel's top line hair, sprays it with 3M glue to hold it in place, then attaches some tufts of white hair to the glue and straightens it. "Little cow toupees," Kathy remarks, adding: "I'm going to work next on Pete," indicating that beneath that baseball cap, Pete could use a little 3M and cow hair.

These are black-and-white Holsteins, but Kathy has used paprika, cinnamon, ice-tea mix, and cocoa to enhance the look of red-and-white Holsteins, Brown Swiss, and red Jerseys.

All the while Kathy brushes and powders and glues, she's whispering sweet nothings to Angel. "You need a gift of gab with humans that I really don't have," she admits. "I have a knack for talking to cows, making them relax and respond to things we want them to."

As the next cow, Lillian, is styled, a slight breeze comes up that disturbs the carefully crafted white powder line on her back. So Kathy reaches into her industrial makeup kit and brings out a large can of shaving cream, which is more wind-resistant. She squirts it along Lillian's back then shapes the cream with a cake-icing spatula. Lillian is starting to look like a dessert entry in a Reddi-wip contest.

Molly is next. She's Maggie's mother, "queen of the herd," and not for sale, but having her photograph available will help sell Maggie, and prove to buyers that she's from a nice family. Molly understandably droops a bit more than the younger cows, although she's still, like, va-va-voom dairy.

Most of Molly's top line is black, and there is no spray powder black enough to match and no black shaving cream. And so Kathy pours black dirt — *potting soil!* — on Molly's back and shapes it with her spatula. "It's the latest thing," she says. Bovine Botox. "We're trying to make them look better than they actually are," Kathy says matter-of-factly.

But isn't there an element here of, like, maybe, sort of . . . false advertising? "When you have your picture taken don't you want to look your best?" she asks. I make a mental note: Rethink Internet/mail-order bride thing.

"We don't go out and just photograph," Kathy explains. "We go out and make pictures. We call it 'cow picturing.' "

Healthy-looking hair is important. And what keeps a girl's hair silky and shiny? Advanced formula Herbal Essence shampoo and conditioner? Well, professional photographer Kathy DeBruin relies on WD-40 aerosol oil. "I think the shinier and cleaner she looks, the more dairy she appears," Pete offers.

Now a few of the cows are having bad-tail days. We all do. All tails are tied with clear fishing line and attached to an off-camera weight to invisibly hold them in perfect, straight position. But some, like Lilly, need tail toupees to give them that Big Tail Look. Double-faced tape is wrapped around the end of her tail and the extension — fall? hair weave? — is slipped on over it. "There's a number of cows that have their tails docked and we'll have to put on a whole tail," Kathy says. She has them in several different colors to match the breed.

You know how mall photographers employ toys and noisemakers to get uncooperative kids to look toward the camera? Kathy uses Pete. He drapes a large camouflage net over his head and most of his body, then shuffles and darts about, stomping his feet, and making strange noises — "oo-oo-ooo-OOO" — to get the cow's attention and to draw her head into just the right position. He rather looks like a woodlands creature that kills summer campers in drive-in movies. Kathy trains these cow distracters to act like this. "It takes them a few cows before they know what they're doing," she says.

She looks into her camera and choreographs: "Work with your feet, Pete . . . That's it . . . Now we're coming . . . Tail back . . . Head up a little more . . . You're turning her a little too much . . . Go away, Pete . . . Go away hard!"

Why the camouflage net, Pete? "The cows would recognize me as a person," he answers. Don't you think the jeans and shoes give it away? "Don't seem to."

The cows must be discussing their experiences among themselves when they go back to the barn, because Pete has to resort to ever more extreme measures to get their attention as the day wears on. He's a bit of a worry at this point, seemingly lost in his role, swinging a shovel and making sounds like the animal-humanoids manufactured in *Island of Lost Souls*: *"Uh-uh-Uh-Uh-UH-UH-UHHHH!"*

For cows with ADD, like Lillian here, Karen gets out the goat. Kermit. "It's the element of surprise," she says, "something to catch the cow's interest when nothing else will." Pete puts down his shovel and picks up Kermit.

"Bring the goat . . . Hold it up, Pete . . . Now back away . . . Head up, Bud . . . Right-front leg back, Nick . . . Telescope the teat . . . Just push it up . . . Leg up, Shannon . . . Back-right leg back, so we can see the udder . . . Push the front teat up . . . Too much goat, Pete . . . Drop the goat!"

At this point it's worth just standing back and taking in the whole scene: there's this cow, and a guy yanking its halter to keep its head up, and a woman spray painting its ears, and tenders assigned to each leg to put it in the right position, and a tail tender to keep that hanging straight, and a scary Thing with a camouflage net over its head holding a goat and yelping. Not to mention the slobber wiper–manure bucket man, who really has to stay on his toes because he's working both ends of this operation.

Kathy retreats once more to her camera.

"Front teat back . . . More . . . Talk to her, Pete . . . C'mon sweetie . . . Head up . . . Tail in a little . . . Clear the grass from her hooves, wanna see her toes . . . Pete, go straightaway . . . Now come around . . . Talk to her, Pete, work her with your feet . . . Tail back . . . Hold it . . ."

The tenders step out, the shutter clicks. "Got it!" Kathy shouts. "Boy, she came around nice. Beautiful!" The camera loves Lillian.

THE BUTTER-COW LADY:
Toledo, Iowa, Pop: 2,539

To me, cows symbolize and embody much of the character of rural life: slow-moving, solid, straightforward, serene . . . almost bovine you might say.

They're kinder, gentler, and just all-around nicer mammals than we are — one reason you never saw Gandhi at an Outback steakhouse. Cows give of themselves and ask little in return. They're laid-back almost to the point of being cool. They seem content wherever I see them, whether crowded in a muddy barnyard in Vermont or grazing on priceless beach-front property in California. They chew their cud and watch Zenlike as we fools speed by on the road, hell-bent for that somewhere next. Could cows be wise?

No matter what the subject of our piece or where we are, I always insist that the crew gets a few nice shots of cows. I've had a life-size plastic cow in my yard for about fifteen years. Why, I can't explain. It's been abducted twice, but keeps finding its way home like those miraculous dogs lost on vacation three hundred miles away. The hard part is calling the police to report the theft of my plastic cow. I think they put me on speakerphone for all to enjoy.

I've done several stories on cows, including two parades, one at the winter Olympics in France, where proud local farmers brought their cows into the town of Moutier to show them off to a world-wide television audience. Another was the Cows on Parade extravaganza in Chicago, where a million visitors came to see 320 artfully decorated plastic cows scattered throughout the city. Cows are a draw, no doubt about it. We've also shot cow-pie bingo in Texas (as part of a larger story). I'm not proud of that.

But there was a cow I longed to see, an extraordinary cow, the incomparable Butter Cow, a full-size representation sculpted entirely from real butter and exhibited at the Iowa State Fair. Once you've seen it you'll never go to the Louvre again.

Artist Norma "Duffy" Lyon sculpts a fresh Butter Cow for the fair every year, slathering a wood-and-metal frame with six hundred pounds of unsalted pure cream butter chilled to forty degrees. I know what you're asking. Well, the answer is: That's enough to butter 19,000 pieces of toast!

Sure, Michelangelo's *David* is good, but could he produce a new one every year? Could Michelangelo complete his in twenty-four hours as Duffy does? No way. Took the guy three years!

Granted, *David* is bigger, seventeen feet high, whereas Butter Cow is five by eight. On the other hand, Michelangelo lived in Florence during the Renaissance, where it was probably a lot easier to create great art than at the Iowa fairgrounds.

Michelangelo apparently never worked in this medium. His choice. There was butter around. There was probably even *peanut* butter by then.

He should have. He should see the herds of art aficionados, among others, standing in long lines in the yawning John Deere Agriculture Building for their turn to file past the big refrigerated showcase that frames the Butter Cow.

During the course of the eleven-day fair, nearly a million people come to admire the Butter Cow at the Agriculture Building — way more than visit *David* in that time period.

That same number, one million, come

to the fair itself — phenomenal in a state of just 2.9 million — and no one would even *think* of missing the Butter Cow. "Our visit is complete," says an admirer with a camera. "We have a picture of the Butter Cow."

Tens of millions have seen it since it was introduced here in 1911, which may have been around the time when the fair also featured two locomotives in a head-on collision! A real shame they dropped that.

The Butter Cow endured. J. E. Wallace, a churned-dairy-spread savant, created that first one and it was so popular he crafted another every year until he passed away in 1956. It would not be an Iowa State Fair without Butter Cow. An interim sculptor filled in before Duffy took over the esteemed (in Iowa) position in 1960 and has produced a Butter Cow every year since.

It's not the same rancid cow every year. Butter Cow is an ephemeral work, created for the fair then melted down and re-created the next year, using the same butter for five years.

How fitting to so honor the cow, without whom there would be no butter! "Were you ever tempted to use Parkay?" I ask

Duffy, as she's doing some touch-ups on her pièce de résistance inside her refrigerated studio-showcase, which looks like a truck trailer but with one side all glass to accommodate the viewing public. "No, it doesn't firm up right," Duffy explains disdainfully, noting that she has sculpted with snow, chocolate, soap, and cheese, but never Parkay. Maybe you can't believe it's not butter, Fabio, but Duffy can.

In comparing the Old Masters, art historians note that Michelangelo did a myriad of works, including the *Pietà* and that Sistine Chapel thing, which I personally regard as more of a trick than art. "Look, I can paint masterpieces on my back."

Duffy too has a diverse portfolio. She has a repertoire of six cow breeds, this year's piece a Jersey. She has sculpted life-size renditions of John Wayne, Garth Brooks, and Elvis, among others. She considers a butter Harley-Davidson to be her best, most intricately detailed piece. Like da Vinci, Duffy has also done *The Last Supper.* Interestingly, there did not appear to be butter on the table at the Last Supper. His choice. It was around.

It is almost as though fate played a hand in this perfect blend of artist and subject.

Duffy and her husband, Joe, are dairy farmers in Toledo, Iowa, who milk 270 cows every day. She took art classes in college. Her great-grandfather, George W. Duffield, served on the State Fair board for more than twenty years. Her uncle Phil Stong wrote the popular novel *State Fair*, which was based on Iowa's quintessential state fair and was adapted for three films and, of course, the 1945 Rodgers and Hammerstein musical.

And the fair hasn't really changed much since. That's what people love about it. They want to see the Butter Cow, the 875-pound pumpkin, the 1st Place sweet-potato cinnamon buns, the longest beard in the state (45 inches), and the grand champion steer. It's standing room only at the accordion contest, there's a long line to see the biggest boar, antique tractors draw a crowd, and the man with the biggest rabbit is signing autographs. A day at the Iowa State Fair is like spending a day in that Rodgers and Hammerstein musical. That was then, this is now, and the twain meet every year at the Iowa State Fair.

POPULATION: ELSIE

MONOWI, NEBRASKA, POP: 1

Coming into the town of Monowi, Nebraska, the sign says the population is two, which turns out to be something of an exaggeration.

The population had been "trending downward" for decades, and stood at just seven during the 1990s. Then the Brockman family moved out, all four of them, followed by the widow, Mrs. Lemons, and the town dropped to two: Elsie and Rudy, a couple about to celebrate their fiftieth wedding anniversary in 2004, when Rudy passed away.

The current population of Monowi: Elsie Eiler. "I am the mayor, the board, the secretary-treasurer, the librarian, the bartender — that's my most important title —

165

the cook, the floor sweeper, the police chief, and I have the books for the cemetery, if someone wants to buy a plot," explains the spunky seventy-three-year-old.

This is self-government as espoused by our Founding Fathers in its purest form, although not really democracy. "I don't bother to hold an election," she says, but she feels good about her chances if she did. So it's really a dictatorship, but a benevolent dictatorship. No complaints so far.

As required by law, she posts notices of upcoming public hearings (open only to Monowi residents), one notice for a recent hearing reading: ". . . for the purpose of hearing support and opposition and questions relating to the one and six year plan for village street improvement." So, I asked Elsie: Did you show up at your hearing to voice opposition or suggest anything to yourself? "No," she answers. "I thought my plan was fine, so I okayed it."

By law, she must prepare the town budget. And how much will Monowi (pronounced "Mono-Y") spend in the next fiscal year? "Oh, I suppose $500 will more than cover it," she says, most of that going to pay the electric bill for the town water pump and four streetlights.

Elsie would also be president of the

Monowi Chamber of Commerce, if there was one. She owns and operates the only remaining business in town, the Monowi Tavern. She basically renews her own liquor license. Interesting, that a bar is the last thing to go.

I had pictured Elsie a lonely soul, sitting out here selling a beer and a burger every three weeks or so to some lost motorist. "No," she laughs, "there's always someone coming or going." Ranchers and farmers come from miles around for coffee (still a dime), for lunch or dinner, or perhaps a beer or two. But mainly they come to chat.

Oh, it can be slow all right. Sometimes she'll get chatted out with someone who's stopped in, and the two of them will just sit there in silence for a long while, not minding at all, as if they're waiting for something. No iPods and no cell phones (which don't work here) to break the silence. "There's a lot of sitting; you've got to be about two-thirds lazy to do what I do," says Elsie, who puts in fourteen-hour days at the tavern, seven days a week.

But it can also get quite busy. This day a crowd of about twenty people show up for lunch, which around here they call "dinner," and it keeps Elsie hopping since she's both cook and waitress. Most of her customers are regulars. Some, like Rocky, don't even have to order; she knows what they want. You don't get a lot of people who are just-passing-through out here since there's really nowhere to pass through to.

They dine on chicken fingers, ham sandwiches, and cheeseburgers. They laugh a lot and chat nonstop about their families, their neighbors, the chance of rain (usually not high), and beef prices (usually too low). Today they're talking about the area high school, over in Lynch, drubbing Verdigre 46–14 in the homecoming football game. They play eight-man football here because they're short on players.

A young delivery man comes in the door carrying boxes of supplies from the outside world. You know how they say a town's so small that "If you blink you'll miss it"? Well, he blinked. "I blew right through," he says, as Elsie pays him cash out of her bulky old register. "I took a photograph of the sign to prove to my wife there's just two people." If he only knew.

If there is an actual middle-of-nowhere somewhere, it might be here, out in central Nebraska on the border with South Dakota, a four-hour drive from Omaha. In the time it takes us to reach Monowi from the East

Coast, we could be sitting at a sidewalk café in Paris. But it wouldn't be the same.

They've had rain and the rolling hills are green with grasses and alfalfa that feed the cattle. The road to Monowi is empty. The town itself is a stark example of the mass exodus that's been going on for decades across the entire Great Plains (comprising all or part of thirteen states from eastern Montana to western Minnesota and south to Texas), as small family farms and whole towns die off like crops after a deep frost. "People are moving out," remarks Gale, a customer at Elsie's. "There are empty houses in the next town just sitting there. You could go over and move right in."

Monowi was never a metropolis, to say the least, but it was a lively little town with a train station, where hopeful settlers arrived and unknowing livestock departed. It sported two banks, two stores, and two bars, serving a bounty of farmers and ranchers.

Elsie's Monowi Tavern is an old one-story structure, painted white (but not recently) on the outside and wood paneled inside. The kitchen is right there, out in the open. There are several tables, and a bar with round soda-fountain stools. Elsie shows me a photograph of men wearing cowboy hats and handlebar mustaches, drinking steins of beer here about a century ago.

It's homey. Folks pay cash, either now or later's fine, as long as it's not too much later. "I'd never heard of paying when you want to 'til I came to a small community," says a thirty-ish rancher named Cannon LeBlanc, who moved to the area from Houston, and whose Dr Pepper and cheddar–sour cream chips are going on his tab.

In the evening (and yes, later afternoon) there's the dinner ("supper") crowd and the beer drinkers. When Elsie gets too busy cooking and serving, they get their own beer. "I tell 'em, 'Don't worry, I can count your empties,' " Elsie says. Regulars also tend bar for her. Mixed drinks are available, but you wouldn't want to order a cosmopolitan or mojito.

It's not a rowdy place. "I have thrown people out," the diminutive Elsie says, "one of 'em physically. He made me mad and he was out the screen door before he knew what hit him." So people know not to mess with Elsie? "That's it," she laughs, "don't mess with Elsie."

And you know how people always say, "You can't be all things to all people"? Well, Elsie comes darned close. She's even been known to do a little short-term day care at the tavern, which explains all the toys over in the corner. She is the core of a community that might not even be a community without her.

"Oh, this is kind of a hub I guess," she says, having not thought much about it. "A lot of people stop in to leave messages for each other and to just pick up something and go on and sit and visit a minute."

Here, where cell phones don't work, Elsie does. She's reliable, doesn't require recharging, and doesn't drop calls. Really she's more of a BlackBerry, a regular high-performance, low-tech information nexus.

Gale comes for coffee on his John Deere tractor pulling a wagonload of hay bales. "My wife, Vi, works in a nursing home," he says, "so if the roads are icy and I want to make sure she's gotten to the highway, I call Elsie and tell her to let me know when Vi goes by."

"Before I get in the door," says Rocky, a welder who's constantly in demand, "she'll holler at me to call home, or she'll say 'So-and-so called and needs you.' She's my secretary and my cook away from home. She's really valuable around here."

Just then the phone rings, Elsie answers it, and tells the caller that the person he's looking for just left on Highway 12 headed toward Verdel. "She does this for everybody," Rocky says.

"You come in," says Cannon (with-the-great-name) LeBlanc, "to find out what's going on in Monowi." So, what is going on in Monowi? "Well, basically, whatever you're doing is what's going on in Monowi. If you want to know anything, just ask her because someone's told her."

Elsie has to agree. "Somebody's probably told me, that's for sure. That's what bartenders get. Everybody tells you stuff . . . sometimes more than you want to know."

Folks post their recent family photos on the tavern walls for all to see, alongside advertisements for goods, such as a Harley for sale, and services, such as "Manure Hauling." And there are invitations to social events, such as a baby shower for the Stroms' newly arrived daughter, Mariah. Here, you don't mail invitations to a baby shower, you put up a notice at Elsie's.

Elsie gives me a tour of her ghost town. The rest of Monowi is falling down or completely gone, except for a nice trailer home she lives in fifty yards up Broad Street, and a new structure attached to the tavern. Elsie is responsible for maintaining the town's infrastructure, and points with pride to the new outhouse out back that replaces two very old, dilapidated, nasty ones — and it didn't cost the taxpayer a cent. It was erected by a motorcycle club that stops here often and had filed complaints with the mayor about the facility so important to beer drinkers.

Just outside her tavern door are the windowless wooden shells of two abandoned general stores, one with a pronounced leeward lean. Walking on up Broad Street, a dirt road that was Monowi's main thoroughfare, she points out the corner where they took down the bank, brick by brick, and moved it to Lynch. Whole houses were picked up and moved, which Elsie says was worth the effort because "some of these were pretty nice houses."

"There's the old jailhouse," she says. Elsie thinks about arresting someone from time to time, "But I'd have to fix up the jail and feed the prisoners, and haul the food up the hill; it's just not worth it." Not the commitment to law enforcement we like to see in these uncertain times, but her approach seems to be working.

Next to the jail is a small white building that's still in use as the town water "plant," or pump. "Every once in a while I have to climb up and read the meter," she says. Then she bills herself (the homeowner and the tavern) and pays herself (the town treasurer).

She says she always pays on time and has never had to threaten to turn off her water. She is a person of many hats and checkbooks.

Up the hill, behind the brush, nestled in two feet of grass alive with grasshoppers, sits a small Methodist church. "My dad's was the last funeral there," she says of the quaint, weathered-gray church. "I guess it will probably just rot and fall down."

The schoolhouse still retains a sheer coating of white paint. "I went first through fourth grades here," Elsie says, "and taught here one year." It's where she met Rudy; he in the fourth grade, she in third.

We walk on what was a street, now covered with grass and wildflowers, perhaps the one Indians called "monowi," or prairie flower. Nature seems anxious to take back the prairie. As people are moving out of the Great Plains, guess who's moving in? The buffalo and all manner of wildlife. "Around here they've seen mountain lions, bobcats, elk, coyote," Elsie says.

We stop at what was surely one of those pretty nice houses she mentioned, it's outer walls still standing, but only the chimney and the collapsed roof inside. "My Sunday school teacher and her family lived here," she says, peering in through a paneless window. I grow a bit melancholy. Not Elsie.

You don't get too sentimental about all this, do you? "No," Elsie laughs, as though acknowledging that she probably should. "You miss the people themselves, but I get along fine. I'm kind of a fatalist, that things are kind of plotted out for us and we have to help them along one way or the other, but there's no need in worrying about what might have been or what happened in the past really."

Elsie is as stoic as her ancestors must necessarily have been, coming to this country from Europe, then by wagon over thousands of miles to settle in this often rather inhospitable climate. And not all that long ago. Monowi was founded in 1902, following the rush of hundreds of thousands of homesteaders who were offered free land, in her grandparents' generation. It has come and gone that fast.

But Elsie doesn't want to dwell on the past. She's looking to the future. In what has to be one of the greatest displays of optimism in the history of civic works, she opened a 5,000-book public library here two years ago! Out front is a sign proclaiming RUDY'S LIBRARY. It's really an old refrigerator door, but you wouldn't know it.

"It was always a dream of Rudy's," she explains, opening the door of the metal shed outfitted with a wooden floor, a little sign-out desk, and floor-to-ceiling shelves of books ranging from *The Complete Works of Shakespeare* to modern-day pulp fiction. "He read all the time," she notes, "and always wanted to get all of his books in one spot." The library also has old magazines and local newspapers going back to the 1940s, the papers carrying front-page articles about Hitler and a successful local tonsillectomy.

Their daughter, who lives in Tucson, says that her father's thought on reading was that a person was never trapped in one place if he or she had books, that one could travel anywhere in the world in seconds by opening a book in even the most remote reaches of Nebraska.

How does this work? I ask Elsie. When is the library open? "Whenever I give 'em the key," she replies. "People come and take books. They bring 'em back and set 'em on the bar in the tavern. A couple of little girls, every time they come they want to go to the library, and that would really please Rudy."

When he died, there was widespread concern that Elsie would move away to be closer to her kids. Folks here don't even like it when she takes a few days off.

"When she goes away to see her relatives," says Vi, "oh my, it seems like such a long time before she gets back here."

And, as Rocky points out, "She has family here. We're all a big family in this area." So he's glad she stuck around? "You ain't kiddin'. We'd be lost without her. I know one thing I'd probably be out of business if she left."

Now I suppose Elsie could put up a new, more accurate population sign. But you know how things go in this town. She'd have to pay for it, then she'd probably have to raise her taxes to pay herself back.

"It's not my duty," she says. "After the next census they'll put up a new sign, probably in 2011."

And you'll still be here?

"Sure! I'm not going anywhere," says Elsie, the beating heart of a dying town.

FIGURE 8 SCHOOL
BUS RACING

BITHLO, FLORIDA, POP: 4,626

The sign says ORLANDO SPEED WORLD, but this ain't Orlando. It might have been Orlando if the combined genius of Evel Knievel and Johnny "Jackass" Knoxville planned it instead of Walt Disney.

The speedway is near Orlando, Florida, but a world apart, over in Bithlo, which the Census tells us is 93.4 percent white, 40 percent without high-school diplomas, and 2 percent with college diplomas. Not that I'm trying to say anything, just that it was perhaps fertile soil for the birth and growth of an exciting new entry in the world of motor sports: Figure 8 School Bus Racing!

This ain't no Disney World teacup ride. You know how an 8 crosses there in the middle? Racing fans, that's your guarantee of an evening of delightful destruction the whole family can enjoy. Tonight's event at the track — Crash-A-Rama — features a slam-bang stock car race and not one but two demolition derbies, plus the main event when the school buses take the track.

"You know how everybody goes to auto races to see the wrecks?" asks Chuck, one of the bus drivers. "Here we do away with all the dull parts and it's all about the wrecks."

Speed World owner Robert Hart invented Figure 8 School Bus Racing. Tasteless. Outrageous. Appalling. Ingenious. Awesome. "When you hear the roar of the crowd sounding like a tornado, you know you've struck the right chord," says this cigar-chomping, Stetson-wearing, nonpracticing veterinarian. "With school bus racing, it's this big ol' thing strutting out for once in its life and running with the big dogs. NASCAR is in the racing business; we're in the entertainment business."

I'd always wondered what these strait-laced, slow-moving, ever-stopping, stop-sign-flapping, yellow-lights-aflashing, stop-at-all-RR-crossings school buses do on their weekends.

This is it. Old buses from all over — their sides reading EATONVILLE CHURCH OF

GOD IN CHRIST, LAKE HOWELL HIGH SCHOOL, DEPARTMENT OF CORRECTIONS, OVIEDO HIGH SCHOOL BAND — are gathering before the race in a lot outside the grandstand. Most are old and battered, although there are a few fairly pristine ones, which the other drivers refer to as "targets."

Most drivers are skilled school bus racing veterans, and some are actual everyday school bus drivers. What a way to work off pent-up aggression from a day of driving a bunch of screaming kids around at twenty miles per hour. One driver is heard to say that he and his fellow school bus drivers have an edge in racing: "I know how they corner, how to get them sideways," which must be comforting to the parents of Orange County.

Another, Jeff, is a tow truck driver in Bithlo and says he gets tired of cleaning up after wrecks and wants to create some of his own. "I don't care about winning," says Jeff, "if you're moving I'm gonna crash you up."

The drivers spend several hours and tens of dollars readying their old racing machines for tonight, inserting a screwdriver for a gearshift on one, tearing out the interior with sledgehammers on another (for a trimmer, faster racing bus), busting out windows, and spray-painting their racing names

— Chuck is "Junkyard Dog" — on the sides. No one works on their brakes.

"I ain't gonna brake 'til I see God!" yells a driver called Red Dog. How'd these guys ever pass driver's ed? Red has his number, 1–800–THE–DOG, helpfully painted on the side of his bus should anyone require his services, whatever those might be.

Another driver, Raybo, sat atop his engine and spoke to the appeal of the sport. "You can go to Vegas and spend thousands of dollars or you can come here and spend $20 and have the thrill of your life." That good? "Yep."

Chuck is a slim, dark, mustachioed driver, about thirty years old I'd say, who accidentally looks hip, with unkempt hair and stubble beard. He's the favorite in tonight's race: a favorite to win because he's won it before; a crowd favorite because he's wedded to this track. In fact, he *was* wedded at the track.

"We got married here," he says, "then that same night we got married we had a demolition derby that I went out and won. That was our wedding reception, a demolition derby." Now if that isn't the *New York Times'* Sunday wedding of the week, you tell me what is.

"I'll probably be in the equivalent of fifty to seventy-five auto accidents tonight alone," says Chuck. "They always told me: 'If you're gonna be stupid, you gotta be tough.' " Chuck drives in the stock car race and a demolition derby tonight as well. That he buys and sells junk cars for a living helps keep him in this game. He points to his demolition derby vehicle and says, "I've got $12 in that car," which appears high.

It's time for a few practice laps and Chuck invites me along. I'm ready to chicken out when two boys, about twelve years old, climb aboard. It's his son C.J. and a friend. (Think before you ask your husband to watch the kids.) So I get on, finding no seat belts and very few seats. The boys prefer to stand, which is fine with Chuck, not an over-protective parent, certainly, who explains that he's been having a bit of trouble with this bus since she rolled over in the last race. The whole vehicle leans to the right. Chuck heads out on the three-eighths-mile banked oval track and has her rolling along about fifty or sixty miles per hour when he yells, "Yeee-haww!" and dives down into the figure-eight part in the middle as the children hold on for dear life. At the intersection we nearly hit the tail of another bus that's out practicing, Dogcatcher. Hey! Rules of the road. Dogcatcher is supposed to yield to the vehicle on his right. "Rule number one," Chuck shouts over the engine's whine, "No rules." The two buses must be going at identical speeds because we nearly hit Dogcatcher again, missing by about a foot at sixty miles per hour, the next time around. (It's like when you run into someone you don't really want to see in the first aisle at the grocery store, and you wind up seeing the person in every aisle in the damned store.) Chuck and I are both laughing now, I nervously, he maniacally.

At the prerace driver's meeting Don, the track manager, tells them, "We want you to try and win, but if you're not the guy who's gonna win, then do me a favor: be exciting!"

"Yeee-haww!" the drivers yell, and out they go to do a parade lap or two before a capacity crowd of six thousand, as always for Crash-A-Ramas.

Sure! Maybe we should all be enjoying a regional theater stage production right now, but hey, it's not like anybody's getting killed (or "kilt") over here. Everybody thinks the Holy Roman Empire was such hot stuff, but they had guys hacking each other with swords and tigers eating area residents as their entertainment.

Chuck helps me put it in context. "What makes this appealing, is that it's something you don't see every day. Anybody can have a demolition derby, but how many people wreck school buses at sixty miles per hour?" Another driver named Mayor offers: "People like to watch buses turn over." Both excellent points.

School bus racing captures some of the free spirit of the old auto racing days, before there were pretty boys who'd attended public speaking classes driving the cars on major networks; before there was a line of NASCAR Harlequin romance novels and NASCAR Elizabeth Arden cologne! (Do you smell burnt rubber?)

This Friday in Bithlo seems a lot like a Friday night I spent at the stock car races in Asheville, North Carolina, where a hotshot from another town had come to challenge the local champ in a dramatic showdown. The local champ's father, also a driver, got right in front of the out of towner during the race and jammed on his brakes, causing the challenger to crash into him. As the local boy cruised past the "accident" to win the race, the out of towner and the father engaged in a fistfight. When this happened we were standing on the roof of the grandstand trying to get a good shot of the track and our veteran producer, Joan Snyder, yelled to the cameraperson: "Shoot that! Roll!" When the cameraperson didn't respond quickly enough, the aging but spry producer grabbed the cameraperson, some thirty-five to forty years her junior, by the arm and shouted, "Shoot that now or I'll throw you off this goddamned roof!"

I liked the Friday night races, especially the fight and the Run What You Brung race, which anybody could enter. A young man raced his father's pristine Lincoln Town Car, which was sideswiped several times and hit from behind. Imagine Dad's surprise the next morning.

School bus racing also has a bit of the feel of the monster truck races we attended over in Tampa, where legendary cameraman Izzy Bleckman was having a tough evening. First he was hit by hard, line-drive dirt balls that fly off the big wheels. He came to me looking quite concerned and said, "We've got a problem. We're shooting the crowd and nobody's got teeth." I liked the intermission when Spanky Spangler was dropped in a car from a seven-story crane onto a van. His chosen profession. And I liked that we ran into him after the races at a nearby Denny's and saw him being hounded for autographs.

And there is much the same feeling here in Bithlo that there was in Naples, Florida, at the Swamp Buggy Races, where a fan told me, "This is as redneck as it gets!" May be.

Naples is now a swanky boomtown, but every so often the old Naples rears its head and roars. Deafening, streamlined, 1,000-horsepower racers with large, thin racing tires blast through a course of muddy water a foot deep — except for the menacing "sippi hole," where the brown water comes up to the driver's chin. Whose big idea was this? Unlike school bus racing, this event actually has historical roots. Hunters used to outfit old trucks with fat, oversize tires and drive them into the muck of the Everglades when they went after deer, wild hogs, and turkeys. This being America, they inevitably started racing their swamp buggies, back in '49, for prizes of turkeys and shotguns. They evolved into finely tuned machines with names like Redneck Rampage and Southern Pride, racing in seven categories as a crowd of thousands cheers them on. Then they throw the beautifully gowned and sashed queen into the swamp.

But enough musing, let's get back to the exciting school bus racing action in Bithlo. And . . . they're off! Not all that fast zero-to-sixty, but once the fifteen buses get rolling they don't slow down for anything. In fact, many do not have brakes. Fans don't seem to care who's winning. This ain't friggin' Le

Mans. Or the Daytona 500. You don't see any Pennzoil-Budweiser-Viagra-Yellow Pages-Cheerios-Nextel-Craftsman Tools-M&M's patches on the drivers' oil-spotted T-shirts. Fans scream and laugh and holler — top-notch incongruity will cause that — as the big fat school buses bump and sideswipe and jockey for position.

They roar around a corner three abreast, banging each other as they head into the 8's intersection and — OOOOOOH that was close! While all eyes are fixed on that near miss, a bus is riding Raybo up into the far turn and — OOOOOOH! Raybo's bus turns over! The red flag is out. Right here I should be writing "The stunned crowd fell silent, prayerfully awaiting word of Raybo's condition," but fans were cheering uproariously! And they cheer again as Raybo emerges from the wreckage pumping his fists. Raybo is all right. Physically.

A forklift clears the wreckage, there's the green flag, and — WHAM! One bus T-bones another at the crossroads! "A real slobber-knocker!" as a fellow fan in the stands puts it. After about fifteen laps of this sweet obliteration, with spent buses sitting in steaming, smoking ruin all over the track, a winner is declared, for reasons we do not fully understand.

But wait! There's more! The speedway holds camper races! "You have got to see this," says Chuck. "The track looks like a hurricane hit a trailer park." And they, too, are off! Very used cars with campers in tow hurtle around the track, and when a car hits a camper, the camper implodes, explodes, and megaplodes . . . disintegrating, indeed, like an off-brand mobile home in a category 5. Kind of alarming, really. I felt like calling somebody at the Consumer Products Safety Commission. "Folks," booms the track announcer, "the owners were still living in that trailer this afternoon." (Hope they're out for the evening.) Some nights everything is blown away but the plumbing, so you'll have a racer pulling a completely empty trailer except for the commode. Talk about a crowd-pleaser.

But wait! They have boat races too! Cars towing speedboats, a whole exciting new form of devastation. Track owner Robert Hart is approaching the status of Vince McMahon — head of World Wrestling Entertainment — in terms of showmanship. And I don't say that lightly.

I ask Hart what's next. He won't say. Hearses? He won't say. I ask if he's considered having schoolchildren on the buses . . . safely . . . you know, with harness seat belts and everything . . . for authenticity. "No," he replies. How about having pictures of kids in the windows? That one, he doesn't answer.

As I go back to watching these old yellow relics of our educational system, driven by and cheered on by products of that system, a question comes to mind: Is our educational system *working?*

MIKE THE HEADLESS CHICKEN

FRUITA, COLORADO, POP: 6,478

Way out in western Colorado, almost to Utah, lies the small but prospering town of Fruita, named for the pears and apples that grew here in the Grand Valley by someone who obviously took Spanish 101.

Fruita has much to recommend it. It's the western gateway to the Colorado National Monument, with its grand sandstone towers and cliffs. It's also a renowned paleontology center, home to the Museum of Western Colorado's Dinosaur Journey. And it has become a hotbed of mountain biking.

So . . . what's with all the folks doing the chicken dance to a polka band, sporting chicken suits and yellow-feathered chicken masks, devouring chicken wings and buying chicken knickknacks, juggling rubber chickens and tossing chicken eggs, and ceremoniously unveiling a new chicken sculpture downtown while totally ignoring the old twenty-foot dinosaur statue that has long and faithfully served as the town's landmark?

The new chicken sculpture is an assemblage of cutting devices — hatchets, scissors, ax heads, sickle blades, and the like — which are appropriate materials because the work depicts a chicken with its head cut off . . . a chicken that's the cause of all this celebration . . . a wyandotte . . . a fryer . . . and a chicken who certainly needs no introduction around here: Mike the Headless Chicken!

The band is playing his song:

Mike the Headless Chicken, legend of the west,
No farmer's axe could stop the heart, beating in his breast.
A sci-en-tif-ic marvel, cuz Mike lived on instead.
Why'd the chicken cross the road?
[Audience] Trying to find his head!

A man with a microphone at this annual Mike the Headless Chicken Festival is reading a proclamation: "Mike, a robust chicken and a fine specimen of a chicken except for not having a head. But such a will to live . . ."

Chickens lose their heads every day, of course, but what makes Mike special is that he didn't let it get him down.

This is their story here in Fruita, and they're sticking to it:

September 1945. Historic times. Japan surrenders to the allies aboard the battleship *Missouri* in Tokyo Bay, and just days later, in faraway Fruita, Colorado, another momentous event is about to take place. Farmer Lloyd Olsen makes a trip to his barnyard and at about 8 a.m. (mountain time) beheads a chicken, not for pleasure or for a Santeria ritual animal sacrifice but rather for dinner. He chops a tad higher than usual, legend holding that his mother-in-law is coming for dinner and likes the neck bone. This strains credulity.

The chicken runs around wildly, like a chicken with its head cut off really, which apparently is not unusual in severe head-trauma cases involving this species. But this case would prove to be shockingly different from any other. This becomes the only known case in the history of poultry medicine where loss of head (not covered by insurance) does not prove fatal.

Mike beats decapitation! Walks it off!

When the chicken is still standing at noon,

Lloyd calls the *Grand Junction Daily Sentinel,* which — hold the presses! — carries the astonishing scoop in the same day's paper.

Next day, Mike is still walking around out there, pecking beaklessly at the ground for food and attempting to preen his feathers. He is in total denial, if that's possible without a brain.

When Mike (why he was named Mike is lost to history) is still alive a week later, Lloyd takes him and a jar containing his head to Salt Lake City, where University of Utah poultry specialists thoroughly examine the bird. They determine that the axe blade missed the jugular and left the brain stem, allowing Mike to live.

They pronounce him healthy, but probably tell him that he might want to keep an eye on the no-head thing. Lloyd feeds Mike small amounts of grain and gives him water with an eyedropper. The two-and-a-half-pound bird thrives, growing to about eight pounds.

"Poppycock," you say? At the festival, I ask an expert, local veterinarian Fred Baylor, if this tale is even possible from a medical standpoint. Fred is dancing the polka in a bow tie that lights up, but he is the only expert I can find. "Yes, it's possible and I'm convinced it happened," Fred says. "The base part of the brain, where your basic biological functions are regulated, was still intact."

"It must be true, it's on the Internet," says Duke, whose Duke's Chicken Kitchen mobile unit is providing the buffalo wings at the festival, where folks come to pay praise to Mike and to eat his relatives. And what finer way to honor someone? "You know how fresh my chicken is?" Duke asks rhetorically, then breaks into rhyme: "From the chopping block to the chicken pot with two stops in between, one for the feathers and one for the inner spleen." Easy to see why he's been so successful.

Many bore witness to Miracle Mike. Local couple Beryl and Jack Oliver saw him. "We were on our honeymoon in Salt Lake City," says Jack, not bothering to explain why, "when we saw Lloyd in a crowd outside a department store. We asked what he was doing and he said he was showing his chicken to people for twenty-five cents, which also included a photograph and a copy of a little poem" — which went: "Although I haven't got a head, I'm better off than if I'm dead." There's a real penchant for chicken poetry around here. "Lloyd let us see his chicken for free since we knew him," Jack continues. "I didn't think it was odd. I guess it didn't register."

"I thought it was something I'd never see," says Beryl. "I didn't think it was possible to live without a head."

"Some people do," Jack remarks enigmatically.

"It put Fruita on the map," Beryl concludes.

Not only did Mike beat beheading, he hired an agent and took his show on the road. Mike signed with Hope Waide, a slick Salt Lake City agent, who took him on a national tour — including New York, Chicago, and Los Angeles — charging twenty-five cents to see "Miracle Mike the Wonder Chicken." Thousands did.

The whole episode is documented in a scrapbook filled with "Headless" headlines (MIKE GAINS WEIGHT), articles, and other artifacts, entrusted to Troy Waters, a great-grandson of the Olsens, who is still farming in the Fruita area.

"This is the scrapbook that my great-grandmother kept of Mike," he says, explaining that, no, she didn't keep scrapbooks for all the chickens. Inside, there's a copy of the agreement Lloyd signed with the hotshot agent that states on the cover: "For the Exploitation of 'Miracle Mike.' " Agents were more direct in those days. There's a nice photograph of Mike with Waide, who is wearing a suit and tie and holding a Ball jar containing a chicken head. "Supposedly," Troy explains, "that's not really Mike's head." The clinchers are photographs and articles in *Life* magazine, which carried a three-quarter-page portrait of Mike accompanying its article, and *Time* magazine, which put Mike's story on the same page with one on J. Robert Oppenheimer, father of the atomic bomb. Mike's article was given better play, spanning the top half of the page, with the Oppenheimer article beneath it.

There are Mike postcards in the scrapbook and twenty-five-cent tickets (fifty cents in L.A.). All those quarters added up. Dirt farmer Lloyd Olsen had the chicken that layed the golden egg.

"He was primarily farming with horse and mule back then," Troy says, "but when he came home from the tour he bought a tractor and all new farm equipment."

Naturally his neighbors envied Lloyd's equipment and several set about trying to duplicate the miracle.

"Fruita was the headless chicken capital of the world in the fall of 1945," Fred the vet says. "Everyone was trying to repeat it. The others lived anywhere from a few hours to several days."

"The Landinis' chicken, named Lucky, lived about a week," according to Teri Thomas, who wrote a (short) book on Mike. "*Life* magazine dispatched a photographer, but the chicken died before he got here."

So what became of Mike? He lived for eighteen months without a head! Then, tragically, like all too many stars on tours, Mike died on the road in an Arizona motel. The little fella was only two years old. Lloyd said they'd forgotten the rubber-bulb device used to clear Mike's throat and that he choked to death.

No one knows where Mike was laid to rest, but few believe he was eaten (this being a culture where we avoid eating those we name) and all agree he lived an uncommonly good life, considering he was born a fryer.

"He didn't end up on the dinner plate and that's where he was headed," Troy says. "He got the cleanest finest straw to lie in. He was fed the finest grains. He was watched after day and night by somebody. You know there's no chicken that gets that kind of attention and Lloyd said he actually saw more of the United States than any chicken in the country."

Right, but Troy, when you say he "saw" more of the United States . . .

"I guess it's more of a figure of speech," he says.

Today, there's the annual Mike festival, T-shirts, the book, a documentary film, a Web site, and a place in the Guinness World Records.

And ultimately, the story of Mike the Headless Chicken is an inspiring tale. You know we all face problems in life, but even when he had his head cut off, Mike didn't let it get him down.

THE MULE TRAIN MAILMAN

SUPAI, ARIZONA, POP: 639

The Grand Canyon is one of the seven natural wonders of the world and Charlie Chamberlain's mail route.

Charlie delivers five days a week to the Havasupai Indian tribe, which resides in the village of Supai, about 2,500 feet down on the floor of the Grand Canyon. Straight down. And it doesn't work to just sort of toss the letters over the side; Charlie has to take the mail down by mule train — the last mule train mail delivery in the country, a mail route opened in 1896.

At dawn — so spectacularly colorful it looks like a cheap, garish painting — the mail is sorted at the Peach Springs, Arizona (pop: 600), post office and loaded onto a good-size truck. "There's only a foot of letters," says postmaster Leroy Hurst, explaining there are about 250 letters, packed tightly, to the foot. "But there's a whole truckload of mail, most of it food."

There aren't any supermarkets inside the Grand Canyon; the closest one to Supai (pop: 639, but I doubt it) is 120 miles away in Kingman, so the Havasupai have their groceries mailed to them. Today there are big cardboard boxes of bananas, tomatoes, milk, Cheetos, Thousand Island dressing, tortilla chips, marshmallows, and frozen meat. Leroy's pretty sure this is the only U.S. post office with a walk-in freezer. Even the milk is frozen so it won't spoil en route through the hot Arizona desert. It's a little costly, taking about $5.27 in postage for a twenty-five-pound box of buttermilk pancake mix, but not too bad considering that's enough mix for hundreds of pancakes.

Now, Peach Springs is already almost all the way to the middle of nowhere, but a young man named Hank drives the truckload of mail seventy miles even farther out, on a deserted two-lane road (Indian Route 18) through a desolate landscape. He sees no other car and not one person the entire trip, except for a lone cowpoke standing by the side of the road waiting for his mail.

There is absolutely no sign of where he might have come from.

Charlie is waiting on Hualapai Hill on the south rim of the canyon with forty or so mules and a few horses when the mail truck pulls in. The horses are not exactly of the show variety; they're working horses that look as scraggly as the mules.

Charlie's not wearing the standard-issue U.S. Mail Delivery Person uniform, but rather a sweater, jeans, leather chaps, and a ten-gallon (37.85 liter) hat.

Charlie's a cowboy, who rides with a looped lasso at the ready. Raised in northern Arizona ranch country, this full-blooded Caucasian married a full-blooded Havasupai and they settled down in Supai. He's been a mule skinner — actually, "mule packer" sounds a bit more PC these days — going up and down the steep walls of the Grand Canyon since 1974.

He helps unload the truck and begins making stacks of boxes in front of each mule, sort of like dads do when they preplan packing the car for vacations. Each mule will carry about 160 pounds. Seeming to know Charlie will be fair about distributing the loads, they stand patiently, on board with his system. No disgruntled postal mules here. One horse is getting new shoes for the trip.

They carry everything imaginable down to Supai: coffeepots, TVs, live chickens — just about anything you can stick a stamp on and then some. "We've carried washing machines," Charlie says, as he hog-ties ungainly piles of boxes on the mules' backs. And they carry the unimaginable. "Even bodies to be buried down there. They might bring 'em up top to be embalmed or for autopsies, then we take 'em back down." Charlie didn't recall what the postage was for your average dead body, but this is probably the only address they're mailed to.

Charlie goes where FedEx, DHL, and UPS fear to tread. "They give us their stuff, they don't go down there," he explains. "No sh . . . kidding," I reply, gazing over the precipice. He straps a bag marked "Express Mail" onto an old mule who seems to chuckle at the idea, although it may have just been a random snort.

It's not what you'd call neat packing, more the worrisome kind you see on top of the car in front of you on the highway. But Charlie carries cartons of eggs on mules' backs right down the face of the canyon and never breaks a one — which is more than most of us can say just taking them home from the supermarket in our SUVs.

It's all fascinating and fun, right up to the

point where I realize Charlie has already strung some mules together in a train, mounted his horse, and that it's my turn. I don't know why, but I'm a little squeamish about mounting a horse in my greenhorn Top-Siders and riding off a 2,500-foot cliff.

I have qualms about mounting a horse under any circumstances. I don't think one mammal should ride another, except perhaps during piggyback races of consenting adults at block parties and company picnics. Equestrian is not my strongest event, yet somehow I wind up riding horses a lot in this job: at a dude ranch north of Phoenix; singing on horseback with the group Riders in the Sky in Colorado; and in my suburban neighborhood on a horse ordered from the Neiman Marcus catalog, equipped with a $125,000 saddle — and a security guard to ensure its rapid return.

As I mount up here atop the canyon, I'm wondering: How *does* a horse walk — or perhaps gallop — down a sheer cliff? Ever see those old photographs of the diving horses they used to have in Atlantic City: riders on horseback diving thirty feet into aboveground pools of water? I fear this might be a similar act, except skydiving horses, plunging 2,500 feet into solid rock. Sorry folks, no second show. Just the one.

Why doesn't Charlie use a helicopter? "This is the most reliable way to get the mail through," he says. "It's cheaper, and a lot of days helicopters can't fly on these canyon rims. Very tricky winds."

And we *do* have faxes and e-mail these days — in the twenty-first century! But so far we still can't fax food and medicine. For the Havasupai, the mule train remains a lifeline. For me, a deathtrap, if only by coronary.

A man named Sun Eagle (we later spotted what was called a sun eagle soaring in the sky) sets out on the trail, leading another train of five loaded pack mules. One of the mules balks and has to be pulled onto the trail. I know how it feels, and wonder if I should break into some hee-hawing.

So off the cliff we go: Charlie, a train of four pack mules, and this uneasy rider, on a narrow, dusty trail, about five feet wide, along the upper lip of the Grand friggin' Canyon! I mean, I'm a flatlander from Illinois where Outward Bound offers climbing the stairs.

The view is spectacular, they say, but I am frozen and staring at the back of my horse's neck. Oh, I probably shouldn't complain. I guess it's really no worse than, say, riding a horse along the window ledges of the Empire State Building, you know? Just higher. But the first time I look up from the horse's mane, the trail is about to take a ninety-degree right turn. Straight ahead is . . . *nothing* . . . that great abyss we've all heard so much about. There it is!

Easy, big fella. My horse doesn't have a name. I guess they don't like to get too close to the animals because . . . you know. If it did have a name, it would probably be Stumbles. He keeps tripping over rocks, and an awful little mutt that accompanies the mule trains up and down the canyon barks at him and nips at his ankles. When the horse hesitates or starts veering a little, Charlie yells, "Kick him!" And turn him into an angry bucking bronco? Not on your, make that my, life.

I look at a box label on the mule in front of me and wonder if we should really be risking our lives for "Crinkle Cut French Fries." I feel a little better when I look at Ray, our cameraman, riding with one or no hands, backward, balancing a thirty-pound camera on his shoulder.

"We haven't lost anyone off these switchbacks in at least ten days," Charlie hollers. Seriously? "Naw," he says, "just kidding." Ever? "Well come to think of it a horse did bump off the trail in January I think it was."

You know that U.S. Postal Service motto:

"Neither snow nor rain nor heat nor gloom of night stays these couriers from the swift completion of their appointed rounds"? Notice there's no mention of the Grand Canyon!

Still, Charlie lives up to that dictum. "In this situation that's the truth," he says. "We're at 5,000 feet elevation, so we get a lot of snow and ice. We still go. We've gone when there was two and a half feet of snow on the trail, and of course in the summer it can be 105, 115 degrees here."

This is fast approaching Evel Knievel territory. Anybody ever ask if you're a little batty, Charlie? "No," he says, "but they've given me some looks, I'll tell ya'. "

Rain doesn't sink into rock, and he's been chased through these canyons by deadly flash floods. "I've been on the trail when there's a twenty-foot wall of water coming behind me," he says. "By the grace of God I was able to get up higher and out of the way.

"And when it rains, rocks like that one slide down," he says, pointing to a boulder the size of a bus. "They make a lot of noise when they fall and it echoes through the canyon."

And to think we complain about the price of stamps! Think it's too high? OK. Here's thirty-nine cents. *You* take this letter cross-country and down to the bottom of the Grand Canyon.

The trail winds its way down through a dizzying series of switchbacks, dropping about 1,500 feet in the first mile before finally leveling off. "Seven miles to go," Charlie announces. But, thankfully, seven much flatter miles.

Now I can relax a little and appreciate the stark beauty of this humbling landscape: the high canyon walls, sporting layers of red, white, and gray rock — limestone, sandstone, and shale. It's a geological showroom. At a distance the walls appear to me to look like (and this is why I'm not a poet) . . . meat . . . a butcher's display case of red, well-marbled beef. The nearer red rocks in the less-than-grand canyons within the canyon are brightly sunlit and set against a deep turquoise sky. Postcard scenes, they're called. Maybe if, say, Matisse painted postcards.

In our three- to four-hour ride we descend hundreds of millions of years. Have you ever walked along a historic street in Philadelphia or Boston and reflected on the fact that people walked on those same cobblestones two hundred years ago? Or walked among ruins that Romans inhabited two thousand years ago?

The kaibab limestone rocks that Stumbles is tripping over at the top of the trail were here more than two hundred *million* years ago. Before there were people, before there was any life on the planet, *that* rock — that one right there — was already here. At the very bottom of Havasu Canyon there is rock, Vishnu Schist, that's been here during the rise and fall of Himalayan-size mountain ranges and the coming and going of countless seas. Staggering.

Charlie is a good tour guide, pointing out a purple prickly pear cactus here, a Spanish dagger cactus there, mesquite trees and wild spinach, and some old abandoned mining equipment from back in the days when they took lead, silver, and nickel from these parts. He tells us to watch for fox squirrel, rock squirrel, bighorn sheep, lizards, and snakes.

But he doesn't have a short answer for how the Grand Canyon got here. No one does. Turns out to be a complicated and not totally agreed-upon answer involving water and wind erosion, continental drift, plate tectonics . . . all that and more. Charlie tends to hold with the uplift school rather than with the erosionists. Empirical evidence: "The canyon floor is a little higher than when I started doing this," he notes.

The rest of the trip is a slow ride, following

a dry wash through sandstone cliffs and listening to the clip-clopping of hooves on crushed rock. I remember as kids trying to make that sound by clicking our tongues when we "played cowboys" on pretend horses.

I come to the sudden, painful realization that the saddle has rubbed all the skin off a silver-dollar-size patch of my lower back–upper butt. I am thirsty and hungry. "Ever sample the goods on the way down?" I ask Charlie, eyeing a big box of Doritos. Charlie says that would be mail tampering, punishable by fines and a prison term. Twenty minutes later I ask, "How many years?"

But coming into view is a ribbon of green, foliage along the banks of Havasu Creek, one foot deep and about eight feet wide, running crystal clear and a preternatural blue-green, like the color-enhanced waters of a mini-golf course. Here it's owing to the mineral content. The creek nourishes a desert oasis at the base of the canyon, its cottonwoods, willow trees, and crops.

Fording the shallow stream, we see that the greenery continues along the trailside. A few wire fences appear. Then some modest houses. But not as modest as mine would be if, like them, I had to carry the boards to build them to the bottom of the Grand Canyon.

The streets of Supai, such as they are, are unpaved. No need, there are no cars and no streetlights — the way it's been since the tribe arrived about nine hundred years ago. A hand-lettered sign notifies riders to keep their horses under five miles per hour, although there is no radar enforcement. Many people keep horses, which they rent to the few tourists who make their way down here, usually by hiking, and they also rent horses to the U.S. Postal Service for the mule trains.

There is a "downtown" of sorts, with a school (K-8th), a Christian church, a small clinic, a little store, a café, and a post office, where Charlie stops the mule train and begins unloading.

He gives the letters to Shirley, the postmaster, then begins untying the foodstuffs, which go to the school, the elderly feeding program, the market, and the café.

Supai is home to about a few hundred Havasupai, who all speak the Havasupai language, and to Charlie. He's lived here all of his adult life, since marrying Agnes, a member of the tribe whom he met when she came out of the canyon to attend his high school in Seligman. They have four children and a grandchild.

Many in the tribe go out of the canyon for high school, and almost all return, some within days, some upon graduation. A few take jobs and try the "modern life" up there, but usually not for long.

"They don't know about money and jobs and cars," Agnes says, by way of explaining her return and theirs.

"Down here we don't have to have money," explains Mathew Putesoy, a member of the tribal council. "You can survive on your own with hunting and gathering and planting corn."

"We grow gardens in the summer," adds Leon Rogers, another member of the tribe, "and in the winter we go to the plateau for game and gathering of wild foods. We go to Hopi land and we trade with them, and with the Navajos." Peaches and corn are exchanged for blankets and silver jewelry.

"I wouldn't like to live in that noisy city with a lot of cars," Leon adds. "I can't even cross the street because it scares me."

"On the outside people are always in a hurry," says Agnes. "They say, 'How are you?' but they don't mean it. Down here when they ask they really want to know. We also come back because we do not wish to neglect or abandon our elders."

Some of them have phones and there are even satellite TV dishes in a few yards. Television puts notions of modernization into their heads, but the elders won't allow paved roads or streetlights or cars or a proposed tramway to bring in more tourists.

"We are the designated guardians of the canyon," says Mathew, who stands opposed to the sightseeing flights above and the uranium mining below. And looking after these guardians are two great rock formations overlooking the village, called "The Watchers."

The light disappears from the canyon as we enter the café, where a sign reads SORRY, NO FRIES 'TIL THE MAIL COMES IN, and I feel like a hero walking in with a big box of crinkle cuts. The fries *must* go through.

The café closes at 4:30 p.m. giving a whole new meaning to "Early Bird Special." It's 4:15, and all that's on the menu at the moment is fry bread wrapped around some red beans — all in all, a deceptive little dish that manages to combine an absolute blandness when eaten with fiery gastrointestinal consequences later on. Discomfort food.

There's a "lodge" down here, which sounds quaint but is not. They couldn't very well call it a motel, since there are no "mos" down here, but that's what it is, a twenty-four-room no-motel usually featuring both water and electricity. The lodge office closed at 5 p.m., unfortunately, but Charlie sees to it that we get our rooms, each outfitted in a minimalist style with a bed, an end table, a lamp, and a commode, but no phone or TV — no sharp objects or cords.

It is 6 p.m., and there is absolutely *nothing* to do. We could call our friends back home and regale them with our experiences in the canyon, but cell phones don't work here. We could have a drink, but liquor isn't allowed. Hello, walls.

Maybe the office has a deck of cards, or something to read. But it remains closed. I peer in the window, looking longingly at a volume of Reader's Digest Condensed Books on a table. Wait! I hurry back to my room and throw open the drawer of the bedside table. But nope, no Bible.

I ache as though I'd fallen the 2,500 feet to get here and decide that soaking in the bathtub would be soothing — and also time-consuming! But, no stopper. Yet by getting into the empty tub and pressing my foot down on the drain while the tub fills, I am able to eke out the semblance of a bath. And! I find something to read: a crumpled piece of paper in my jeans pocket containing some information on the story we're doing, Charlie's home phone number, that sort of thing. So I read that . . .

Next morning, the calm is broken by the whacka-whacka-whacka of helicopter blades, which kick up clouds of thick dust that engulf the village. Four tourists step out. The tribe makes a little money from tourists by charging them camping fees and selling them a few provisions.

They come to see four spectacular waterfalls that make this place a Shangri-la. Heading through the desert about a mile out of town you suddenly hear the incongruous sound of rushing water, the rapids in Havasu Creek. And then Havasu Falls, where twin torrents roar over red rocks before plunging 106 feet into a lush pool. Nearby is Mooney Falls, which at nearly 200 feet is higher than Niagara Falls and more spectacular than anything imagined by the watermeisters of Las Vegas.

"We call them the mother of waters," Mathew says. "We believe that when we pass away our spirits fall down in the waterfall and dance back up and down again, and they are singing and dancing. They are very sacred.

"We like things down here the way they are," Mathew says. "Natural."

The sparkling blue-green waters that flow

through this desert paradise make their way to the muddy Colorado and out into the modern world.

Charlie Chamberlain leads our mule train out of town, on the mail route that many here say allows them to preserve their cultural identity, separating and insulating them from all things modern.

As we head up the trail, another mule team coming down in a cloud of dust is led by a young man riding tall in the saddle — Jeremiah, Charlie's son.

Stopping for the night in rural Kansas, I ask the motel desk clerk if he can recommend the best place in town for dinner. He scratches his head, thinks about it for a while, and says slowly, "Well . . . I'd have to say the Texaco, 'cuz the Shell don't have no microwave." But thank God for those gas stations with their little food stores. Frankly, microwaved sandwiches leave me cold, since the melted plastic wrapper always seems to become part of my sandwich, but a dinner of Chee-tos (crunchy), Slim Jims, and a Budweiser "40" can seem like manna from heaven when there's no other food around.

We often roll into a town after all the restau-

Kathy DeBruin, bovine photographer

The author foolishly challenges the World Watermelon Eating Champion

Author lands interview with huge white squirrel!

Helen makin' Moonburgers

rants (or the restaurant) have closed (9 p.m.), and are left to dine at the motel vending machine: the M&M's complemented by a plastic cup of bathroom tap water is a popular choice. Or dinner might be all the little crackers and nuts in all the little dishes on all the tables and on the bar in the lounge.

Dining on the road is a perilous, deep-fat-fried adventure with alternating bouts of starvation and binging. It takes a lot of fortitude, Imodium, and Zantac to push on — especially after the "Adventure Platter" in a Sunnyside, Washington, Mexican restaurant. But we've also dined at places like Jean-Georges' Prime Steakhouse at the Bellagio in Las Vegas, where the seafood tower appetizer alone cost seven days of my CBS per-diem meal allowance, breakfast, lunch, and dinner.

And I recall a romantic dinner at a nice hotel, when room service brought up fine cuisine on a clothed table set with a rose and two wineglasses — and I was there alone in my underwear watching a hockey game. Perhaps if I'd order less wine and food there wouldn't be such misunderstandings.

And I recall a balmy evening in an enchanting beachfront restaurant in Santo Domingo, a full moon rising over the Caribbean, the water sparkling, a faint breeze blowing, as I am sipping a daiquiri, looking across the table and thinking: Why am I here with Bud Lamoreaux? I really like Bud, a senior producer at that time nearing retirement, and I suspect he was thinking the same of me that enchanted evening.

For breakfast, some of the newer chain motels like Hampton Inn offer a complimentary breakfast in the lobby — the ones where you fight traveling retirees for that last Danish. Beware: they can be dangerous when they're wielding tongs.

Lunch often just doesn't happen. One of the first and only things I was ever told about the TV business was "Eat when you can," because you're never sure when the time and place will be right again. As a backup, we carry power bars that taste like dirt.

We drive-thru a lot to save time. There is an art to eating in a moving vehicle, one that has been perfected by many California motorists but not by me. There I saw a driver deftly eating a bowl of cereal with milk while steering with her knees; another was eating unwieldy crispy tacos at seventy miles per hour that I cannot successfully consume at a stationary table.

My favorite drive-thrus — better than even drive-thru funeral homes and wedding chapels — are the daiquiri drive-thru stands in

Louisiana, where you drive up, buy mixed alcoholic beverages in Styrofoam cups, and drive off sipping them through a straw. Outrageous, but true.

My favorite drive-thru moment occurred at the Dairy Queen in Branson, Missouri, where we were doing a piece on a contest to determine the Accordionist for the New Millennium at the Lawrence Welk Resort. It was one of those days when it got to be four in the afternoon and we hadn't had lunch yet and everyone was getting surly. So I drove our road family's minivan into the Dairy Queen drive-thru lane and at the pickup window the manager handed me our order and bellowed, "I thought it was you! I could tell by your voice when you ordered. Love your show. You're a class act, Bill, welcome to the Branson Dairy Queen." I think that last line is one of the funniest things anyone's ever said to me.

When traveling in the hinterlands, it is important not to have high, or even reasonable expectations. "You call this gumbo?" our cameraman snaps at the young waitress. Shocked, she can't answer. "This isn't gumbo! This is vegetable soup! I've had real gumbo in Cajun country!" Fine! But now we're at the Lafayette, Indiana, Holiday Inn. Meat loaf would be the better choice. This is like ordering sushi on Monday in Scottsbluff, Nebraska.

Having no expectations lets you in for some wonderful surprises. In Buffalo to do "Buffalo — an Appreciation" ("Wouldn't you like your city better if half the people left?"), we happened into the Anchor Bar, where buffalo wings originated. In L.A. we came upon "The Home of The French Dipped Sandwich," the Philippe restaurant, where Philippe himself accidentally dropped a sandwich — roast beef on a French roll — in the pan juices in 1918 and the rest is history. There was the fantastic homemade boudin at a gas station in Cajun country; a sublime grilled fresh fish sandwich at an out-of-the-way seaplane landing in Key West. One of the great moments in my own personal road-food history occurred in Wiscasset, Maine, while doing a piece on an antique-shop owner who was selling a priceless (but not to him) 3,000-year-old Egyptian mummy. It had created an international incident, with Egyptian officials up in arms, demanding its return, and the U.S. Customs Service ordering it impounded. Being from Maine, the shop owner said he'd sooner throw it off the Sheepscot River bridge than turn it over to anybody.

And next to the bridge sits a bright red shack with a sign emblazoned RED'S EATS where you can walk up and order the best lobster roll in the world, each one containing the meat of more than one whole lobster. Then you savor it on Red's little deck overlooking the Sheepscot. The mummified Egyptian queen (who only later turned out to be a king because no one had looked) never had it so good.

Traveling as a crew of four, there are frequent disagreements when choosing a restaurant for dinner. "That looks good," said our camera-man, pointing to a $3.99 Chinese buffet. "No!" the producer and I barked, as one.

We're in a town where two restaurants are highly recommended, but there's a wait of a good half hour at both, and our cameraman (and driver) won't wait, so he drives on, passing other restaurants that look overly popular until coming to one that certainly is not. "Now *here's* a good restaurant," he says, wheeling into the empty parking lot. "We can park right here in front." Which, of course, turns out to be its only asset. The Michelin restaurant guide does not give extra stars for convenient parking.

Sometimes a chain is the best you can do. At least at a Bob Evans the food looks like the picture. There are times when you're thrilled to come upon a Cracker Barrel, where you can have the chicken-fried steak (with cream gravy) with three sides (turnip greens, fried okra, and cheese hash browns) and they bring the defibrillator paddles right to your table.

Some in our road family like buffets, others do not; it's an issue that continues to divide this country. Myrtle Beach, South Carolina, is one of America's buffet capitals, sporting buffets as lavish as their mini-golf courses, which we saw while doing a piece on the Masters of Mini-Golf, won by Team Sweden. One buffet touts "126 items!," another competing buffet also "126 items!" Why doesn't one of them just introduce a 127th? Maybe 126 is all the food items there are. Perhaps there's a state law setting legal limitations on buffet items to protect the structural integrity of buildings. But it becomes a moot question when we pass a seafood buffet with 170 items! That's got to include, like, pond-scum polenta. They must have had to start making stuff up.

Las Vegas was built on cheap buffets back in the '50s and '60s, along with cheap rooms and complimentary cocktails for gamblers. Vegas is truly Buffet World and Olga Scheel, the reigning "Queen of Las Vegas Buffets." She takes me to see the awe-inspiring one-hundred-yard buffet at the Rio, with more glass in its sneeze guard than Reverend Schuler's got in his Crystal Cathedral. While stuffing shrimp into her purse at the sumptuous Paris buffet, Olga explains that people out here have buffet strategies. "You come in just before the breakfast hours are over, you grab breakfast, then eat lunch. So you're in there eating for hours for the low price of a breakfast." At Main Street Station, buffet manager John Carlson marvels at how much even skinny seniors can consume. "We have T-bone Tuesday, which is all the T-bones you can eat. They're one-pound T-bones and a few customers have eaten seven."

As everyone knows, at a buffet there's "No Sharing"; says so right on the sign in the Holiday Inn restaurant in Indianapolis, where our family is staying for a reunion. I come down for breakfast, see my sister-in-law Sharon in a booth, and join her. As we're chatting and waiting for my menu, I eat a couple of pieces of bacon from her plate, whereupon an aging waitress in a rural 1890s getup, comes over, bends down, puts her face inches from mine, and says quietly, "I seen what you's-a-doin', you little shit-ass."

Tips for Travelers: Restaurant Warning Signs
1. "Family Restaurant"
2. "Fine German Dining"
3. Restaurant also sells gasoline
4. Next door to animal hospital
5. Designated "Ambulance Only" parking spaces
6. "Valet Parking" attendant doesn't issue

claim check, speeds off onto highway

7. Seated next to couple oblivious to their three noisy brats . . .

8. . . . and mother is delivering fourth on the table as they finish dessert

9. Ask waitress for recommendations and she replies, "Leave!"

10. Ads on placemats for angioplasty specialist, obesity clinic, Pepto-Bismol, and grief counseling

11. Menu sections: "From the Sea"; "From the Land"; "From the Asphalt"

12. Today's asphalt special is the "Mixed Grill"

13. Preview your meal using helpful food samples splattered on menu

14. Each table has individual Roach Motel

15. Silverware bends like Reynolds Wrap

16. Excessive praying: Diners saying grace before every bite

17. Double cheeseburger, large fries, and super-shake combo designated a "Heart Smart" selection

18. Chip tooth on meatloaf . . . rabies vaccination tag

19. Server shows flair in cutting open plastic microwave meal bags tableside

20. Notice sign on the way out: "TO HELP SAVE THE PLANET, WE RE-CYCLE LEFTOVERS"

ROADKILL, THE MAN, AND OTHER GOURMANDS

OUTSIDE OF TOWN, KANSAS, POP: SPARSE

The Alferd Packer Memorial String Band (named for the noted trail guide and cannibal) plays at the Lawrence, Kansas, post office — *inside* the post office — every year on April 15 to brighten the spirits of last-minute tax filers, some of whom sprint in with their returns seconds before midnight.

It's turned into quite a party, with balloon animals for the kids and free food for all — although the postmaster, who's wearing a Hawaiian floral shirt, says it's probably gone as far as it can go. She doubts she'll ever be allowed to serve margaritas.

An aproned man stands behind a serving table outside the post office dishing up dinner for a couple of hundred people who

225

show up for the festivities. What's for dinner? I ask. He says it *was* wild turkey and dumplings, but that's all gone. "But there's still plenty of these," he says, motioning to a chafing dish and a large soup pot. "I'm Michael Coffman," he says, putting out his hand, "but everyone calls me Roadkill."

Oh. And . . . why is that? "Well," he replies, "because I'm on the sheriff's list and when a deer gets hit on the road — or when I was in Idaho if an elk got hit on the road or a moose — they call me and I go out and harvest the animal while it's still fresh." And, I ask, what do you do with it? "Eat it!" he replies.

"This here is roadkill stew," he says, stirring the soup pot. "This is what I'm famous for. This year its special ingredient is Alaskan musk ox."

Where'd he get that? "I have a friend who's a doctor in Alaska," he answers, ambiguously. He says the stew also contains some elk, venison, turkey, duck, and goose.

So, is that . . . ? I start to ask, pointing to the barbecue in the chafing dish. "Yeah, that's groundhog. There's his head, his skull. I left that in there so you can tell what you're eatin', and to prove it's groundhog." It's all part of Roadkill's quality assurance program.

Any varmints you won't eat? "It's hard to

get a good-tasting skunk," he notes, which sounds plausible. "And possum is so greasy I won't even hardly pick one of 'em up anymore."

So, the groundhog was hit by a car? "Yeah," he says. "Got clipped. You can see the head's crushed. My cousin saw it get hit on the highway and he stopped and field-dressed it and threw it in the freezer.

"All you have to do is beat the flies to it," he says. That's his secret and his pledge to you, the consumer.

"Roadkill is plentiful, with everyone building houses and all the cars," he says optimistically, making roadkill sound like a leading economic indicator.

With the little skull in there, the rectangular chafing dish sort of looks like a Georgia O'Keeffe, painted during her barbecue-sauce period. Are people actually eating this? "They will," Roadkill replies with confidence. "There won't be none left."

What does groundhog . . . taste like? "Tastes like pork," he says, "tender and moist like real rich pork."

He offers me a taste, and with a crowd egging me on, I take a plastic spoonful. I thought, "When in Rome," and then I thought, "No, in Rome I'd be dining on *saltimbocca alla romana* with a nice Chianti.

I am in Kansas, about to eat baked and bar-becued Punxsutawney Phil."

So this is real roadkill? "Yes it is," he says. What road? "Highway 24. And we think it was Michelin tires that got it." Michelin! Haute cuisine!

I spoon it into my mouth, trying not to think of rodentia, and begin to chew, and chew, and chew — but can't seem to swallow.

"Well, what do you think?" Roadkill asks enthusiastically. Best I ever had, I reply. And it is.

Sometimes food *is* the story. Our mothers told us not to go swimming right after eating, but they never mentioned anything about flying in a small plane on a windy day after eating enchiladas and black beans.

Pilot Dave Heffernan wrote a guide to fly-in restaurants in Oklahoma. You know, the state where the wind comes sweeping down the plain? We've just dined at Enrique's Mexican restaurant in the Ponca City air-port after flying in from a huge breakfast at the Runway Café in Wiley Post Airport in Oklahoma City. Now it's on to Ozzie's at the Norman airport for Ozzie Burgers, which are essentially grilled heart attacks on a bun.

"You want to have something to do with

your airplane," Dave explains, "a purpose for going out flying." Our next meal is all the way down along the Red River, the border with Texas. The headwinds are so strong that we're barely keeping pace with the crew car on the road below. Dave makes his approach and I can't help but ask, "Where's the runway?" We land in a field and bounce along to a stop adjacent to the McGehee Catfish Restaurant.

I ask Dave: What differentiates this landing strip from a cow pasture?

"Well," he answers, "most pastures are leveler, wider, and there's less obstacles on them." But Dave does seem a bit concerned when we take off, owing to my consumption of hush puppies. And it *was* our fourth meal of the day.

He's thinking of widening the scope of his guide a bit, so we next fly just across the border to the very small town of Beaumont, Kansas, for dinner at an old hotel. We land among the cows, then in a real surprise, Dave taxis right down main street, stopping at a stop sign and everything, before pulling the plane into five parking spaces in front of the old hotel. Unfortunately, the hotel is closed, perhaps forever. But Dave seems not at all perturbed. I think he knew it was closed.

■ ■ ■ ■

Sometimes when food's the story it can be bad news. Madison, Minnesota, is the Lutefisk Capital of the World, as it proudly proclaims on the sign when you drive into town. Bet there are a lot of U-turns made at that sign. The literal translation of lutefisk from the Norwegian is "lye fish," fish soaked in lye — you know, that stuff in oven cleaners with a warning label saying if swallowed call 911 immediately.

Lutefisk is said to be a Norwegian delicacy, invented by Vikings, who took dried codfish on their long voyages and soaked them in lye water to plump them back up. In truth it's a slippery, slimy, smelly, and highly controversial dish. That anyone would take its side is hard for me to believe. Some describe it as "fish jello" (a flavor not under consideration by the Jell-O corporation). "You could put it under your porch to drive away cats," suggests one woman, trying to remain positive. But then you'd have an infestation of Norwegians under your porch.

At the Lutefisk-Eating Championship (where I finished second in a field of two in the novice division), no condimentation of any kind is allowed and rules stipulate that the lutefisk must "stay down" for at least one minute. A blackboard is placed on the stage between the contestants and the crowd, serving the same function as a baseball backstop — and baseballs aren't hurled much faster than lutefisk.

On the audience side of the blackboard there is entertainment while the rounds of eating are under way. Some local girls are singing "I Will Survive," but they're not the ones eating lutefisk. Lutefisk Queen Ivy Vanderharr walks through the audience greeting her subjects, while perennial champion Jerry Osterhaas (in Minnesota, it always looks like the keys are sticking on my computer) left his challengers gagging in the dust for his tenth title.

THE TOURIST HARVEST

OLNEY, ILLINOIS, POP: 8,470 (ET AL.)

America doesn't make much anymore. It's too much *work,* too much heavy machinery, too much noise and smoke. These days we sell, we trade, we deliver, we type, we upload and download, we feed, we entertain.

In rural areas, struggling family farmers coast-to-coast are turning to "agritainment," cutting elaborate mazes in their cornfields where people come out and pay to get lost. Maize mazes, hayrides, pumpkin patches, petting zoos, and U-pick-'em fields. One wily farmer I met was having New Yorkers pay for the privilege of being bused out to pick his vegetables. Now *that's* good.

Here's what a lot of small towns like to do. They like to get out of towners to come, then they feed 'em lunch, let 'em look around, sell 'em "antiques" and dream catchers, and send 'em back where they came from. It's called tourism; fast, easy, clean money.

But first you've got to figure out how to bring 'em in. If you're a small town and don't have a Statue of Liberty or a baseball team or beaches or maybe a big rock with presidents' faces carved in it, you have to get creative. Of course, they can't all be as fortunate as Kokomo, Indiana, which pulls 'em in with the biggest sycamore tree stump in the world and packs a one-two tourism punch with the biggest steer that ever lived, now stuffed.

Make your town the capital of something, anything really. Or open a museum. Or hold a big festival. Or come up with an attraction of some kind. Don't be bashful. Americans are easily amused.

Olney, Illinois, among others, calls itself Home of the White Squirrels. Since we're on the road in our big RV and headed in that direction, we call ahead and arrange to meet someone who can tell us all about it. We're to meet in a park where a lot of these white squirrels frolic. The person we talked to never shows, but luckily a six-foot white squirrel that walks on its hind legs and talks does.

"White gold," says the giant squirrel. "That's what they call us here because we bring in so many visitors." Really? "Yes, we surely do. We bring in busloads of squirrel watchers."

If white squirrels are white gold, Olney is their Fort Knox, protecting them with all manner of laws and inalienable rights. "It is, of course, illegal to kill or injure a white squirrel," explains a burly police officer. "It is also illegal to harass a white squirrel." Harass? So, you could call a brown squirrel "a little nut-sucking bastard," but not a white squirrel? That just doesn't seem right.

"It is illegal to take a white squirrel across city lines," he says. Even to dinner or a movie? "Yes, that would be a violation."

Cuero, Texas, and Worthington, Minnesota, both claim the title "Turkey Capital of the World," even though about the only turkeys you'll find around either town anymore are Butterballs. Cuero started its turkey fest in 1912, and historic photographs do show ranchers driving thousands of the birds through town on the way to market.

The two communities hold a home-and-home turkey racing series every year, where their fastest turkeys race each other down the main streets of both towns. The winner based on total time becomes the turkey capital for the following year, although it should be noted that Berryville, Arkansas, also claims the title.

Thousands are drawn to the races, which are wild and challenging to TV crews, given the fact the turkeys have no idea where this whole thing is going and neither do we. On race day Cuero's sidewalks are packed six deep as the two caged turkeys — Paycheck (because nothing goes faster than a paycheck) from Worthington, and Ruby Begonia from Cuero — are ceremoniously brought to the starting line. You can almost hear a bugler's call to the post.

Anxiety sets in. I suddenly realize we've flown from New York to Houston, then driven three hours to Cuero, and we just might not be able to capture this wholly unpredictable event on tape. Our crack crew, Mike Hernandez on camera and Cleve Massey on sound, only get one chance at what amounts to a poultry jailbreak. (Lord knows it's not like the wiener dog races in Buda, Texas, where they taped hundreds of those graceful thoroughbreds competing for two whole days.) Amy, our producer, has her golf cart waiting midcourse to pick up Mike so that he can shoot back at the approaching turkeys. That's the plan.

And they're off! Paycheck darts out to an early lead, but then veers into the crowd. Mayhem ensues. Ruby suddenly shoots off down the street straight toward the finish line. Amy floors it to get out of Ruby's path. Mike runs past me, his camera bouncing on his shoulder, his eye nowhere near the viewfinder, and I'm certain we're doomed. Ruby streaks across the finish line. Somehow through the magic of television the crew has captured it all.

Hold a festival! You can do it! We've stopped at the Kumquat Festival in Dade City, Florida; the Dean Martin Festival in Steubenville, Ohio; and a yam fest in Opelousas, Louisiana.

Sometimes a festival is just what the doctor ordered to raise morale and, perhaps, money. Opelousas had held its annual Yambilee for sixty years, but wasn't going to have it in 2005 because of the wreckage of lives and property left in the wake of Hurricane Katrina. Four hundred New Orleans evacuees were sleeping in the auditorium normally used for the festival: the Yamitorium. (A bronze plaque confirms that this is its official name.)

But at the last minute townsfolk decided it was important to carry on their tradition, so everybody pitched in and made it happen. It would have been a shame not to. Yambilee has a rich history; dignitaries like John F. Kennedy have come down for the parade.

Opelousas is all about yams, which they tell me are sweet potatoes given that sobriquet to differentiate Louisiana's from all others. And they're everywhere: in the fields, on the menu every day at the Palace Café, and lurking unseen in hundreds of local dishes.

The festival's Yam King this year is yam farmer Blaine Joubert, who was coronated at a yam mass in the local Catholic church. Paige Broussard is Yam Queen. The royal couple rides on a yam float in the yam parade with Queen Yum-Yum, King Yum-Yum, Mr. Yam, Junior Miss Yam, and Yam Teen Miss, among others.

Sue Deville is proud to have been one of the Yamettes, also known as the Yambassadors, a troupe of young women who used to travel near and far as cheerleaders for the tuberous root. She shows me her old cheerleader-style uniform and a copy of their (local) hit: "The Yambilee Song."

There's yam music and yam poetry, too. Queen Paige, in her crown and long, sequined, yam-bedecked train, delivers a dramatic reading of one poem that ends ". . . as an abundance of sweet potatoes falls to the ground; amazed at his magnificent yield, the farmer calls them his . . . jewels . . . of the field."

Holding the festival was important to the town and also to the yam itself. Yams need the recognition. They get no respect. George Washington Carver made more than a hundred new products out of yams: inks, dyes, even synthetic rubber. But all anybody talks about is those damned peanuts.

Maybe the yam just needs an image makeover, a PR campaign like "The Other White Meat," "The Incredible Edible Egg", and "Got Milk?" How about "Yams: They're Under the Marshmallows"?

Open a museum! Go on.

Museums need not be stuffy places with security guards and boards of trustees. And you don't need much to work with. Nothing is so humble or mundane that there's not a museum display case for it somewhere in America.

There's a Museum of Dirt! Curator Glenn Johanson greets me wearing a white lab coat. I always like a white lab coat. It says "credibility." I expect him to say, "Four out of five doctors recommend dirt."

I thoroughly enjoy the museum, but then I

once had to drive from Chicago to Georgia, and collected dirt from every state along the way to make my girlfriend a mud map labeled "Muds I Saw on My Trip." Her father looked at the mud map and commented, "There's a fine line between humor and insanity."

The Museum of Dirt, in Boston, is really more of a gallery of dirt, with hundreds of glass bottles on display containing dirt samples from around the world. And it's not all brown. There's blue dirt from Blue Earth, Minnesota, dramatically displayed next to pink dirt from Hurley, New Mexico. Most visitors are drawn of course to — what else? — the *celebrity* dirts: dirt from Vanna White's backyard, from LBJ's birthplace, Jerry Vale's sculpture garden, Barry Manilow's driveway (which you'd think would be paved), and from the set of *Baywatch,* sent in by David Hasselhoff himself!

Or so they say. There is no easy way, dear reader, to authenticate these samples, but Glenn does have on the lab coat, so . . .

Glenn may have been kidding a little with his museum, but Bill Beeny is not. He's the curator of the Elvis Is Alive Museum in an unassuming little wooden building in Wright City, Missouri. He may well look like what Elvis would look like today: packed tightly into his white bejeweled jumpsuit and wearing big aviator glasses, he's a little jowly, with thinning hair and long sideburns dyed black.

Beeny first shows me a book entitled *Elvis' DNA Proves He's Alive,* adding, "DNA proof; can't get any stronger than that. The living Elvis you see here," he explains, pointing to a photo on the book cover, "was not the same person as this individual (also shown) in the casket." And I have to say: they do not look alike.

He hands me an audiotape. "This tape has Elvis's voice on it, telling why he faked his death," he says, leading me to the next exhibit: a coffin with a body in it.

"Here we have reduplicated Elvis in the casket," he says, gesturing to the dark-haired, pockmarked, painted (Styrofoam?) head. "Some have said, 'Well this doesn't look like Elvis,' and I say, 'That's correct. Neither did the individual who was in the casket at Graceland.'" (Indeed when I've visited Graceland I have not sensed his presence.)

There's a nice reproduction of Elvis's so-called "grave site," one of Elvis's cardigan sweaters, photos of his wedding to Priscilla, and souvenirs such as a framed Elvis portrait, rendered on black velvet, which I could not pass up. There's also a small café where

Elvis's favorite sandwich, grilled peanut butter and bananas, is served. "Elvis would eat six of these at a time, all the time," Bill says, as I enjoy mine. And you know, he had me convinced that Elvis might very well still be alive until he said that.

Anybody famous born or live or sleep or stop for a pack of smokes in your town?

Huntington, Indiana, opened the Dan Quayle Center and Museum for its favorite son, featuring Dan's law degree with a bite taken out of it by the family dog, Barnaby; one of the former vice president's business suits; and a green curtain from Dan and Marilyn's first home.

(Hey, that's better than Bill Clinton's hometown, Hope, Arkansas, which apparently didn't anticipate greatness and tore everything down. On my visit, all they had was his boyhood home and one cousin, Margaret Polk.)

In Huntington, I took a brochure and hit all the stops on the "Quayle Trail," seeing his boyhood home and his high school (where he starred on the golf team), and eating where Dan ate. Nick's Kitchen now serves Quayle Burgers, but I voted to skip that because there's a sign that says this is home of the "World Famous Breaded Tenderloin."

Huntington is not kidding, and I'll tell you who else isn't: Elizabeth Tashjian, the loveliest curator I've met, she of the Nut Museum in her Old Lyme, Connecticut, home.

The slight, elderly, sharp, sprightly woman immediately breaks into song. "There is a museum devoted to nuts . . ." which is the beginning line of the third verse of her "Nuts Are Beautiful" homage. Other of her recordings (perhaps not distributed, but recorded) include the "Nut Anthem" and the stirring "March of the Nuts."

Here she introduces the visitor to hundreds of nuts from around the world, ranging in size from the barely perceptible to a thirty-five-pound lunker from the Seychelles, a coco-de-mer. (My best guess is that coco-de-mer may mean "hot chocolate made with salt water" in the Seychelles Creole dialect.)

Elizabeth had even more nuts before a recent break-in. "Chipmunk vandals and squirrels," she says, shaking her head. "Eating the exhibits."

She displays nut paintings, one a surreal work depicting nutcrackers and nuts floating about in peaceful harmony. (That'll be the day.) There's nut jewelry and native nut masks and nut carvings. "Gauguin carved nuts," she reminds me.

Elizabeth can't say enough good things about nuts. "You can never feel lonely with nuts around," she says, quite rightly. "They keep you occupied and the sound of cracking nuts spells party."

Sure, we all agree that nuts are interesting and educational, but she says nuts are fun, too. We go outside and play a game she calls "Rolling Eyed Coconuts," hitting croquet-ball-size nuts with sticks, beneath her nut trees. She wins.

Moreover, Elizabeth Tashjian firmly believes that man is descended from nuts. And who's to argue?

While traveling the country in a big RV, we stopped at the RV hall of fame and museum and library in Elkhart, Indiana, where RVs dating from 1913 are on display. Some of the units are shown in realistic settings with fake folks sitting around a campfire outside their RVs. Some are luxurious, with mahogany interiors, two bedrooms, and spacious kitchens. We can trace the advent of the pop-up camper and the coming of the Winnebago. There's a library for RV scholars and a hall of fame featuring the giants of the RV industry, such as Wally Byam, the founder of Airstream, and Mahlon Miller, credited with the innovation of the slide-out family room.

Ironically, Miller is said to be Amish and cannot ride in RVs.

We have a slide-out room on the one we're driving, and we pop it out as soon as we stop for the evening. This night we have an excellent campsite: the Wal-Mart parking lot. Wal-Mart welcomes RVs to park overnight free in their lots. We shop for snacks and things in the store, then return to mingle in the lot with our neighbors, who are pulling in for the evening. Pat Albert is formerly from Canada but has lived for five years full-time in his forty-footer. "I don't like to be too long in one place," he says. He showed me how to put out my awning, which was right neighborly of him. "It's nice out here," he remarked. And as I sat on my folding chair drinking a beer watching the sun set over the Wal-Mart lot, I had to agree. It was a little piece of heaven on wheels all right.

Another thing small towns do to jump-start tourism is to identify (or possibly sort of make up) something distinctive about their communities.

Chestnut, Illinois, proclaimed itself the Geo-Center of Illinois. "Geo-Center" just sounds so much more . . . *now* . . . than "the middle of," doesn't it?

A young out of towner discovered this by

hanging state maps from his basement ceiling and drawing plumb lines, which seems rather unscientific, but lo and behold, a team of scientists at the Illinois Geological Survey confirmed it.

The community rallied around this intangible, invisible new fact. "Everybody just went crazy when we found out," local resident Gene Blue tells me, "and we've had soup suppers and pork-chop-sandwich dinners, and everybody comes."

They built a Geo-Center Monument with $6,500 raised from the sale of commemorative bricks, and held a big unveiling bash with bands and proclamations and dignitaries, who got a little carried away, calling it "the geographical center of Illinois," "the United States," and "the world." The little store that has provided basic provisions to local folk for many a year stocks a line of souvenirs — hats, bumper stickers, shirts — and they are moving fast.

Alas, there is no joy in nearby Illiopolis. "Ever since I was knee high to a grasshopper," says a disappointed Frank Pritchet, owner of the Showroom Lounge in Illiopolis, "we've always been the center." He blames the whole thing on computers. Interesting. I leave wondering if he just might be right, and also wondering if he has any problem booking lounge acts in a town of nine hundred in the middle of nowhere — and now no longer the center of anything.

Did anything of historical significance ever happen in your town? Like what? Like the Battle of Gettysburg, or the pilgrims' landing, or the filming of *Field of Dreams*?

As James Earl Jones's character put it in the movie:

People will come, Ray. They'll come to Iowa for reasons they can't even fathom. They'll turn up your driveway not knowing for sure why they're doing it. They'll arrive at your door as innocent as children, longing for the past.

For reasons I can't even fathom, tens of thousands of tourists every year do come to a baseball diamond carved out of a cornfield, where *Field of Dreams* was filmed. Kevin Costner isn't there anymore. Neither is James Earl Jones. Just a baseball diamond.

On a back road outside Dyersville, Iowa, you run across two signs and two separate unpaved driveways. One sign reads LEFT & CENTER FIELD OF DREAMS with a big red arrow inscribed ENTER HERE; the other,

ORIGINAL FIELD OF DREAMS MOVIE SITE. The driveways run parallel just a few feet apart. Farmer Al owns the left field and center field; farmer Don owns the farmhouse, diamond, and right field. There isn't an invisible fence or anything to shock visitors who stray between the two properties because there's no admission charge. But each driveway leads to its own souvenir and refreshment stand. The two farmers are not on the best of terms. Now you'd think Don's house and diamond would have it all over Al's two-thirds of the outfield, but Al's left field has the corn — the magic cornfield in the movie from which the old players like "Shoeless Joe" Jackson appear and disappear, in their uniforms and young again. Sometimes Al has players in the old uniforms come out of the corn and play catch with tourists. He did that for us, even though the corn hadn't even been planted yet and the ballplayer came out of the field of dirt.

The most famous line from the movie is "If you build it, he will come," most often quoted as "If you build it, *they* will come," and which I've found to be true about 90 percent of the time. Towns build goofy museums and people come. They build biblically themed miniature golf courses, where I got a hole in one on Noah, and people come. They build whole domed stadiums *on spec,* and professional baseball teams come. Everybody's looking for something.

SILVER SURFER

SAN ONOFRE, CALIFORNIA,
POP: VARIES

Doc Paskowitz is a *serious* slacker. You can find a lot of slackers on the beaches of Southern California, but none compare to Doc.

With the exception of a few part-time jobs, he's spent his whole life as an unemployed surfer, not unheard of among your top slackers, but this man has been doing it for sixty years! He graduated from Stanford's medical school — then became a full-time surfer! Now *that's* impressive.

I was growing up in landlocked central Illinois when the surfing tsunami hit the California coast in the early '60s. But the Beach Boys were coming in strong on my transistor radio:

If everybody had an ocean
Across the U.S.A. ˏ
Then everybody'd be surfin'
Like Californ-i-a . . .

But, of course, we did not have an ocean. I didn't see the ocean until I was twenty. We could, however, sport surfer-wear. We could lace up the surfers' low-cut black "Connies," Converse All-Star basketball shoes, which was the only athletic shoe brand around in those days before Nike-Reebok-Adidas made cross-training, walking, and sitting-on-your-fat-ass-watching-TV shoes. Usually our stores carried only white Converse high-tops.

You'd see 'em wearin' their baggies
Huarache sandals too
A bushy bushy blonde hairdo
Surfin' U.S.A.

A few adventuresome corn-belters began showing the long, bleached-blond surfer hair. Both genders. (We only had the two back then.) A few who had some connections to the West Coast wore baggies. No one went with the huarache sandals, footwear that could get you beaten up in the Midwestern and Great Plains states.

We never knew the thrill of riding a wave. Didn't really have thrills as such. We knew that something was going on in the warm California sun, because our fellow Americans were packing up and moving out there by the millions. Something exciting, rebellious, even a tad revolutionary. But we didn't quite get it. We still aspired to successful white-collar jobs, modern ranch homes, attractive spouses, and Buicks. But somehow these California surfer dudes didn't seem to be . . . *on board.* Their brains baked by the sun and eroded by salt water, their highest ambition (if you will) seemed to be hanging ten, hanging out — just generally . . . hanging.

And so, years later, it's still something of a cross-cultural, foreign-exchange experience, when I meet life-long surfer and überslacker Dorian "Doc" Paskowitz, seventy-six, on San Onofre beach in San Clemente . . . still surfing.

Doc is indelibly tan, one of those sixty-years-at-the-beach tans that can darken the skin pigmentation of future generations, the kind that can cause secondhand tans to those around him. Probably, his organs are tan.

He is boyish, barefoot, and fit. He wears tan shorts and a jean jacket over a white polo-style shirt, just like the kids in the Abercrombie & Fitch catalog. His short hair is gray (but so is Anderson Cooper's). His face is creased from years of squinting.

"I've been down here since I was fifteen, right here!" he says, standing on the beach with arms outstretched toward the sea. "I paddled out right here. How many surfers were out that morning? Me and one other guy. Now look. Two hundred!"

He first went surfing in 1920 in his hometown of Galveston, Texas, and must have *really* enjoyed it is all I can say. How did he even think, in 1920, to take a tree or whatever out in the waves and try standing on it? Doc didn't actually invent surfing, as some on this beach contend. Somebody else did that hundreds of years ago out in the Pacific isles. Why is unclear. Probably some shipwrecked soul desperately clung for life to a piece of the hull for days without food or water, miraculously washed ashore, stood up in the shallows and yelled, "Kickin', bro! I'm stoked!," then paddled back out.

Doc finished med school in 1945. "I toured the world and surfed for ten or fifteen years," he says. "I wrote a book called *Surfing and Health,* health through diet, exercise, rest, recreation, attitudes of the mind — and surfing." The doctor prescribes surfing, megadoses of surfing.

In 1956, in a Catalina Island bar, he met a tall (six foot two) Mexican-born singer named Juliette. They married and hit the road in a camper in 1958, going beach to beach, surfing and having children, surfing and having children. Doc is often called the "Father of Surfing," which seems apt since he's raised nine of his own kids to be surfers, plus a passel of surfing grandchildren.

Nowhere in any childrearing book does Dr. Spock or any other expert suggest raising nine children in an eight-foot-wide, nineteen-foot-long camper, but that's what he and Juliette did.

"The funny thing," says Juliette, a statuesque and, some might suggest, saintly woman, "was when we used to pull up to a beach and the door would open and from this small camper kids would start pouring out and they'd keep pouring out and they wouldn't stop." Like circus clowns from a minicar. Where did they all sleep? "Overlapped," she answers.

They are the world's first family of surfing. Navah is the only girl. The eight boys are Izzy, David, Abraham, Moses, Adam, Jonathan, Joshua — all Old Testament, except Salvador. "I think I was the first Jewish surfer," Doc explains.

It's a handsome lot, which is no surprise after you meet Juliette and see photographs of Doc as a younger man, buff and posing in his swimsuit before a big, old, heavy-duty surfboard.

The little camper was not only home to this nomadic band of surfing gypsies but their school too. The kids were camper-schooled, an obscure form of alternative education. "Never went to school," says Sal. "All I did was surf and read books as a kid. Navah's read every book ever written by anybody."

"Reading's all we had to do," she explains. "We didn't have television, we didn't have electricity."

How has Doc pulled this off? Did Juliette have any idea what she was getting into when she signed on with him? "Absolutely not a clue," she says. "Not at all. No idea. All I could see was those blue eyes."

She wanted to be an opera singer, but says, "I sang to my children, that was fine, that was enough." Does she ever feel as though she sacrificed her dreams, because he wanted to surf? Every day! Forever! "No," she answers emphatically. "When someone shows you paradise, it doesn't have to be your notion."

Financially, of course, it's been hard.

Sometimes in order to make ends meet, Doc would take temporary, part-time jobs in local clinics and hospital emergency rooms. Yet Doc has turned down Nike endorsement money, as well as a family inheritance.

"We had seven bucks in our pocket," he recalls. "I had been given an inheritance of $70,000 by my aunt. And I said to myself, 'Now look, I am the happiest man in the world. Don't shake the boat, don't rock the boat; give it back.' Well, the court made me see a psychiatrist, and the psychiatrist said, 'Paskowitz, listen, I'll sign the affidavit, but believe me, you're crazy. You're nuts!' " A professional diagnosis.

Finally Doc figured out a way to make his passion pay: Paskowitz Surf Camp! The idea was inspired by a glum realization when the oldest son, David, turned fourteen, that one day soon his children would grow up and leave the home/nest/camper. But with Surf Camp, they could stick around as paid camp counselors and instructors.

The plan worked. Even now, all of them grown, the kids return every summer to work at the camp, and they bring the grandchildren.

"He always says he dropped out of society and into his family," says Moses, a strapping former college football player. "I love that.

Dropped into surfing as well. And that's what keeps us bound together, keeps bringing us back."

Moses has just arrived at the beach and Doc rushes over and kisses his biggest boy on the lips. A lot of hugging goes on among all the family members. The Paskowitz Mobile Box experiment seems to have bonded them, rather than making each of them flee to separate remote deserted islands or making them set fire to Winnebago factories.

Izzy, a former world champion and professional surfer, runs the camp, which opened for business in 1972. "This is what I love to do," he says, "introducing new surfers to the sport of kings." Isn't that horse racing? "No," he says, "surfing was big with royalty in the South Seas."

About twenty campers per week, most of them "kooks" (complete novices), come throughout the summer to camp out and learn to surf. They become part of the Paskowitz family, a self-described "bunch of crazy half-breeds, Jewish and Aztec."

At a picnic-table orientation, various and sundry Paskowitzes explain to arriving campers that surfing is more than an outdoor leisure-time activity. "You're flying on water," Jonathan tells them. "By riding a wave, you satiate your desire to be free."

"Surfing has not only a physical but a metaphysical, spiritual factor," is the message of Moses. "Surfing is healthy for your mind, body, and soul. I guarantee you if Elvis surfed he'd be alive today."

And finally Doc: "If this comes off right, you'll understand what we feel . . . it's very difficult in life to talk about the meaning of a kiss or a mother's love or surfing. Go out there and catch one wave. It doesn't have to be forty feet high; one little wave, and something will happen to you, inside."

As temporary members of the family, campers are instantly plugged into bohemian surfer culture. They are immersed in surf-speak. They ride around in a big old blue bus adorned by amateur painters with big waves and hula girls. They take field trips to places like the San Onofre Shop, where they learn about boards and waxes and surfer trading cards — one of which happens to be an autographed Jonathan Paskowitz.

After a full day at the beach, the funky bus takes them back to a state campground, where they dine together at a long, homemade picnic table, talk surfing around the campfire, and watch surfing videos. Occasionally a surf camper decides to camp out at the Ritz-Carlton Laguna Niguel instead; occasionally one eschews the healthy choices at camp meals, and goes off to Pedro's Tacos.

There are religious services, and even those take on surfing overtones. Doc dons a green yarmulke on Friday nights and conducts a Shabbat service that is decidedly nonorthodox. "Hey, it's a great day," he prays. "This is the day that God made. Let's really go out and surf. And thanks for the food. Hit it!" Then everyone sings a prayer in Hebrew. "We lived in a camper together for twenty years," he explains later, "so we had to make up our own rules."

Most of the campers have never tried surfing before. And despite a good deal of on-the-beach instruction, particularly in the three-step method of standing up on the board, it doesn't come easily even on the smooth, rolling surf at San Onofre.

"We've never failed to teach a camper to surf," brags Doc, who's taught thousands. That could change today. Camper Mike is out in the water falling over again and again, as might be expected of a slightly paunchy forty-nine-year-old, gray-bearded postal worker from Denver, where surfing conditions are just terrible. He's wearing an orange T-shirt over his wetsuit, which should make things easier for the Coast Guard.

Camper Andrea, nineteen, is also falling a lot. She's from New York City, where the closest thing to surfing is trying to remain standing on the subway. Camper Jeff paddles too slowly to catch a wave, and when he does, it isn't pretty, even though he's from California. Must be Sacramento or someplace. Doc admonishes him: "Take a more aggressive stance like a boxer, not a victim about to be mugged."

But Bill and his daughter Kirsten, campers from Florida, are good. "This is our twelfth year coming to this camp," he explains. Kirsten is getting married and has a prenup that she can return to Surf Camp each summer with her father.

Doc has returned to shore after an hour or so of gliding effortlessly over the waves as Juliette sat on the beach, content to watch. Doc observes his campers and staff through binoculars, letting out a cheer when he sees Andrea up on her board.

Mike prepares to go out and try again. "I mean this with the utmost respect and affection," he says, pointing to Doc, "but if that old coot can do this I'm sure I can." He paddles out with an instructor. Doc stands at water's edge watching him intently and muttering "Oh too bad" time and again, before finally a "Here we go . . . Uh-oh . . . OK . . . He's up . . . Now hold it!"

Mike appears petrified, his legs straight

and wooden, his arms out as stabilizers, and looking rather like a statuette at a Christian gift shop. But, God bless him, he's staying up! "Atta-boy!" Doc shouts.

He falls, as all surfers eventually must, and stands in the surf, whooping with joy, pumping his fists, then just standing still with a broad grin as Doc laughs and whistles and claps.

The sun is going down over the Pacific, and the waves are rolling in, cresting and crashing. Another surfing day is done.

THE MUSEUM OF TOWING

CHATTANOOGA, TENNESSEE,
POP: 154,762

In Chattanooga, Tennessee — OK, sometimes I do go to the big city — there are some must-see attractions, like the famous Choo-Choo and the legendary Rock City that we used to see advertised (SEE ROCK CITY) on barn roofs all over America.

But they're not why we're here.

We venture into Chattanooga, the big, but not all that big, city because sometimes a story speaks to you, calls out to you upon hearing but a few words: Tow Truck Museum.

But wait. It gets better: The Tow Truck Museum . . . and . . . Hall of Fame. Forget Cooperstown. Let's go.

It's the International Towing and Recovery

Hall of Fame and Museum, to be precise. And, lo and behold, it really is a full-blown museum dedicated to tow trucks and tow persons, financed by a group called "Friends of Towing," which sometimes we are (in the ditch, in a snowstorm) and, frankly, sometimes we're not (two wheels barely in No Parking zone).

It's a big showroom crowded with shiny old tow trucks, some going back to the '20s and '30s, some most attractive, with gleaming chrome grills, voluptuously curved fenders, running boards, and polished wood dashboards. Indeed from the front these tow trucks look like luxury cars from the black-and-white film days. You could pick up not only disabled vehicles in these babies but Greta Garbo as well.

Frank Thomas is the genial, grandfatherly host. The man has a passion for tow trucks. Are people surprised, Frank, to see a towing museum? "Yes they are," he replies. "They come in and ask, 'Is this for real?' "

On display are the first tow truck, tow trucks through the years, and special tow trucks like the mini Japanese model for towing smaller cars. There is a towing library with bound volumes of *American Towman* and *Tow Times* magazines, and towing videos.

The museum houses towing artifacts, such as an antique quilt depicting tow trucks, and celebrates great moments in towing history. A color photograph shows a 177-ton something or other, an earthmover maybe, that went off the road and down the side of a hill in South Africa, and the five tow trucks and two bulldozers making the recovery. What a job!

There's a U.S. Army tow truck. "That one was used in World War II," Frank says. "It helped win the war. That was one of the wrecker's finest hours I believe."

It's a shrine that treasures tow trucks. As our camera rolls, Frank is in the midst of delivering his spiel to me about a truly glamorous '29 Packard, when he stops mid-sentence to scold, "You're touching the door."

Frank says about ten or twelve thousand people visit the museum each year. There's some now, a couple from Michigan. "We were looking at brochures at the welcome center and one of them was for the towing museum," says she. " 'What's that?,' I asked. 'Tow trucks,' they answered and I said, 'You're kidding me.' "

"I think it's great," says her husband. "I think it's time they got some recognition." The back of his jacket reads "John's Towing

Service, Coopersville, Michigan."

A young woman named Asuka traveled by train from Boston to Atlanta, then caught a bus to Chattanooga just to visit the museum.

"My father owning towing company in Japan," she says, and shows us a photograph of his truck. "He really love towing trucks like crazy. His birthday in a few days so I decided to come here and take pictures and get souvenirs." Plenty to choose from in the gift shop: towing books, toys, mugs, needlepoint, yo-yos, air freshener . . .

The question visitors often ask is: Why a tow truck museum?

And why in Chattanooga? "This is where it was all started," Frank says, "by Ernest Holmes, who built the first twin-boom wrecker and patented it in 1916 just a block and a half from where we are now."

There's a photograph here of that first wrecker. "He cut off the back half of a 1913 Cadillac touring car," he says, "and put in the towing unit." Bold.

Frank, do you think people come here on towing tours to see the birthplace and the museum? "Oh yeah!" he says.

A deluxe Chattanooga towing tour package could also include the site where Ernest Walter Holmes Sr. invented the tow truck, which is already designated by a historical marker. Then on to the scene of the momentous accident that started it all, where the story can be told: In 1916, John Wiley's Tin Lizzie flew off the road and landed upside down in Chickamauga Creek. Wiley was OK, but it took Holmes and five other men eight hours to get his car out. Vowing never to go through that again, Holmes returned to his garage and invented the tow truck.

After a light lunch, the tour could continue at the world's largest tow truck manufacturer, Miller Industries. "We look at the towing industry here in Chattanooga as what the auto industry is to Detroit," says Miller vice president John Hawkins. "This is the tow truck capital no doubt about it."

He's a member of the Tow Truck Hall of Fame, and so is Frank Thomas, who shows us walls of inductees, towing professionals from some sixteen countries, the giants of towing. The Hall of Fame is something a young tower named Jeff over at Yates Towing aspires to. "You need to be someone who has been in it for a long time and does outstanding work at reasonable rates. I just try to be nice, you know, to go out and do my job and not scratch or dent. I don't know if that qualifies as Hall of Fame, but that's what I try to do, be the best that I can be."

We want to accompany Jeff on a towing

call. As we wait in the office for a call to come in, one of the employees says, "Jack-knifed tractor trailer."

"Really?" I say excitedly, imagining what great TV this is going to make!

"No," he says quietly. "Be good though."

Yes, yes it would, but we had to settle for a small old BMW that wouldn't start in a mall parking lot.

Back at the Hall of Fame we ask Frank if he considers tow truck operators unsung heroes. "They're unsung heroes, yes," he answers. "They're the first ones out there to help people get out of the ditch, rain or shine, night or day."

He says the museum's purpose is three-fold: to preserve towing's rich heritage, to provide towing education, and to honor unsung towing heroes like pioneer Ernest Walter Holmes without whom the wheels of the entire world would still be spinning in the muddy ditches of time.

BOAT CHURCH AND OTHER OUTDOOR SPORTS SECTS

SYRACUSE, INDIANA, POP: 3,030 (ET AL.)

It's a summer Sunday morning on sparkling Lake Wawasee, aswarm with speedboats, Jet Skis, water-skiers, Windsurfers, swimmers, tubers, and fishermen — heathens all.

They should be in church, these hedonists, but who wants to get all gussied up and sit in a pew on such a fine day as this? Churches face serious attendance problems in the summertime.

But the Right Reverend Harlan Steffan has one solution: take church to them. He casts his boat upon the waters, boards another one anchored forty feet offshore, and from this pontooned pulpit delivers the word of the Lord. The Lord Himself, of course, would have just walked over.

On this sunny Sabbath day on Lake Wawasee in Syracuse, Indiana, a flotilla of the faithful gathers, a congregation of several hundred bobbing and slightly rolling worshippers in 150 to 200 boats and on one Jet Ski. And that's not counting a couple of fishermen who were listening in and about a hundred more sitting in lawn chairs on the shore. No one ever swam to church, but many have come in kayaks and canoes.

As boaters arrive for church, most dressed in swimsuits, an usher in a boat of his own greets them, "Morning," and passes them church bulletins clamped to the end of a long pole. The cover of the bulletin is blue and reads "Bridge over Troubled Waters."

"Good morning," says Reverend Andrew Hardy, the warm-up minister, from the pontoon boat, equipped with a microphone and speakers. "Welcome to Boat-In Worship . . . Let us pray: Heavenly Father we thank You for this opportunity to worship under Your sanctuary, under Your skies, upon Your waters . . ."

Reverend Steffan delivers a sermon with an aquatic theme, invoking Noah and the crossing of the river Jordan. Then the Covenant Brothers quartet, accompanied by an elderly woman on the keyboard, sings: ". . . step into the water way down a little bit deeper . . ."

Reverend Steffan explains that the idea was inspired by the biblical tale of Jesus preaching at the Sea of Galilee. Boat-In Worship is now a joint program of the Presbyterian Church, Church of the Brethren, the Nazarene Church, the Church of God, and a Mennonite church. A pontoon boat of Mennonites is out cruising about on the lake this day, the women in long drab dresses and white aprons, the men with their beards, plain hats, and long black coats — but wearing sunglasses. Probably for practical reasons, but they appear to be stylin' a little.

Boat church does present a few unique problems. One Sunday the minister fell in, but they could always pass that off as a total-immersion baptism. And what about all of the distractions out here? Do worshippers really get the message with outboards whining, ducks swimming, and girls in bikinis skiing by?

It's certainly more casual. Many listen with their toes dangling in the water. Some parishioners drink coffee and eat doughnuts. One is cuddling his girlfriend, another lying in his swimsuit with his eyes closed on his boat's prow. It's possible he's still there from Saturday night and isn't aware he's at boat church.

I ask some of the boaters: Do you think this counts? I mean: Is this real church? "Absolutely," say the Dumfords, Sue and Dave, who brought coffee and doughnuts and their dog, Cassie. "It's inspiring," says Dave. "It gets us close to nature and that's what God's about."

Boat church, which started in 1970, draws more worshippers every year and is even spreading to other area lakes. "It's really growing," says boater-worshipper Sharon Wible. "This year we have to get here about half an hour before the service starts to get a good parking spot on the lake."

In winter, heathens ski.

A skier riding the lift on Copper Mountain in Colorado seems to have a quizzical look as he peers beneath him at a group huddled together singing . . . a hymn?

"On a hill far away, stood an old rugged cross . . ." they sing, against a calendar-perfect backdrop of vivid blue skies, snowy peaks, and evergreens.

"I like the cathedral," says Reverend Dub Chambers, pastor of ski church, taking it all in.

Ski church, where the faithful schuss, carve, and plow to slope-side services in full ski regalia. So, too, Reverend Chambers, who says he had to learn fast to ski when he was assigned to the Copper Mountain Community Church. (I once took what they called a "crash course" in skiing, and I learned crashing well.)

Worshippers plant their skis and poles in the powder and the reverend leads them in prayer: "We ask You, Father, today, as we ski, that You may be with us. And may this white snow remind us that we are truly covered by Your grace."

The congregation sings a cappella, because no one really wanted to lug a pipe organ up ten thousand feet. Worshippers recite the Lord's Prayer. And with skiers cruising by, Reverend Chambers delivers his own sermon on the mount.

He says a lot of people still can't quite grasp the concept of ski-in church. "People will ask, 'You mean it's outside? Outdoors?' And I answer, 'Well, yeah. It's outdoors like the Lord did it, you know? Most everything he did was outdoors.'

"Sometimes you hear things differently in a different setting," the reverend says. "You get used to a routine, traditional service where the message is always the same."

"It's nontraditional," says Corey Geiger, in attendance at the service, "but that's what I like. I like it casual, relaxed, you know. Not stuffy."

Three boys, all probably about fourteen years old — James, Anthony, and Marshall — make it to ski church.

"It's short," James says appreciatively.

"It's kind of weird seeing the priest in ski boots," Anthony observes.

"It's good to thank God for all this snow," James adds.

"I think skiing is a very spiritual thing, honestly," says Marshall, raising the plane of the conversation. "You feel so small compared to the mountains. You realize how insignificant you are."

"Up in the mountains you feel closer to God," adds another skier, Jack Rose. "And you are."

Heathens surf, too. But wait, these Sunday-morning surfers are not heathens; they're true believers who go to church every Saturday evening so they can catch the Sunday-morning waves. "I'm sure God understands," comments one who's "stoked on Jesus."

"Welcome to Surfer's Chapel," says Reverend Bill White, standing behind a pulpit that's a sawed-in-half surfboard. He addresses worshippers not in silk-and-velvet robes, but rather a wild polyester Hawaiian shirt. The congregation numbers about fifty people, most of them wearing floral Hawaiian shirts too.

"Surfer's Chapel," he repeats for emphasis, "where Jesus is Lord!" And the congregation responds loudly in unison, "And we surf on a board!"

Here, at a rented chapel in Huntington Beach, California, surfers park their boards, taking a moment to thank and praise the Great Wave-Maker. "We're Surfer's Chapel, so, you know, it's pretty much come as you are," explains the minister. "Just knock the sand off your feet before you come in. We literally have people who come in with a damp pair of trunks and their hair still wet.

"We're Christians," explains Reverend Bill, who has long blond surfer hair. "We're just kind of in a different wrapper."

He reads from 1 Corinthians 3:10. Then a four-piece band — three guitars and a drum — plays an old tune, "Surfer Joe," retrofitted here with new lyrics: *"Went down to Huntington Beach one week, to the Surfer's Chapel where the Christians meet . . ."*

The weekly church announcements are a bit different, too. "Stevenson Diaz turns fourteen tomorrow," Reverend Bill says, "and he got a new board. Get up here with that new board." The young man comes forward and shows his new board to a shower of "Cool"s.

The sermon is entitled "Shaping Your Board and Your Life."

Back at Lake Wawasee, boat church is over for another week. The catch of the day is cash, which they land by passing the old collection net. I'm not calling it a naval blockade, but you really couldn't get your vessel out of there without passing that usher, who this time has a fishnet on the end of the pole.

Reverend Steffan does not fall in. I ask him if he misses the steeples and the stained-glass windows of a church.

"The warm sun rising, the water sparkling, a light breeze blowing, it all lifts your heart and your spirit," the minister says, glancing at a sailboat gliding silently by. "No, this is the greatest cathedral in the world. Right here."

FLAMINGOS IN PARADISE

CELEBRATION, FLORIDA, POP: 2,736

Disney World is a nice place to visit, but would you want to *live* there? Two thousand people already do, in the town of Celebration, Florida, a perfect small town built from scratch by the Disney company adjacent to Disney World.

You never have to leave the Disney property to get from Disney World to Celebration — in mind or body. A road leads straight to it, which sometimes leads to confusion, according to one young man who lives there. "My mom was in her pajamas coming downstairs to make coffee. All of a sudden these people walk in. She goes, 'May I help you?' And they go, 'Oh, no, we're just looking around.' And she goes, 'This is our home. We actually live here.' And they wouldn't leave." Probably figured Mom for an animated character.

New residents happily sign a 166-page Declaration of Covenants restricting just about everything that might conceivably annoy anyone, ever; sort of a personal, formal, legally binding Declaration of Non-Independence. And they're pleased that all of their neighbors have signed it too, so that there won't be any surprises. The document bans the planting of non-designated shrubs, limits the choices of visible window treatments to white or off-white, and mandates prior approval of any change in house color. If your dog barks too much it can be permanently removed by the authorities. No more than two individuals may sleep in any one bedroom, pretty much doing away with kids' sleepovers — not to mention three-ways. Boats and RVs are to be kept in back and out of sight with the recyclables.

It's a modern-day utopian community, along the lines of those created by the Shakers, Oneidas, and Inspirationists — except their covenants were with God rather than the Disney Company.

More than fifty-two million Americans and counting now live in these "private common-interest communities" or "master-planned communities." You know, the kind where people ask each other: "Are you in Phase II or Phase III?" Many millions of these people live in the popular gated communities, which despite the gates and the guardhouses (no guard *towers,* yet) don't offer much security, really, but do seem to provide a feeling of exclusivity. (I would note, however, that I have spotted a couple of gated trailer parks.) I was once in a nice gated community when I noticed another set of gates: a gated community *within* a gated community. This must be helpful to thieves in determining where the really good stuff is.

Celebration is a whole master-planned *town,* a picture-perfect, pastel town of charming neo-traditional houses drawn from the designs and sensibilities of Charleston/Savannah/New England-inspired houses. Buyers may choose from six different home styles. Some have faux dormers and faux second stories, but in no case do you open the front door and walk into the backyard, Hollywood style.

I spend my life celebrating the individuality of twenty-first-century man, then something like this happens! Celebration, Florida.

So, six styles of houses, but there's pretty much just the one style of human: of a sort attracted by orderliness and cleanliness; searching for a haven from the unraveling of social fabric in the outside world; and nostalgic for a return to happier, simpler, safer times. This type of man cannot realize he is safer now from crime (violent and property) than he has been for decades, because he watches television newscasters ("Bird Flu!" "Mad Cow!" "Grisly Murder Someplace!") and listens to politicians ("Terror!" "Terrorists!" "Terrorism!"), both of whom depend for their livelihoods on keeping us scared to death.

Celebration isn't all bad by any means. The houses have front porches and are built close to the sidewalks to encourage human interaction — that is, talking. The houses are almost all built within walking distance of downtown to encourage walking. The fact that there even *is* a downtown sets it apart from a lot of newer "communities." There's an office complex for working and a hospital with a name that almost makes you glad you're sick: Celebration Health Campus. And there does seem to be a sense of community here, in part because everybody agrees to agree on everything before they move in. From the sales brochure:

There once was a place where neighbors greeted neighbors in the quiet of summer

twilight. Where children chased fireflies . . .
There is a place that takes you back to that
time of innocence. A place where the
biggest decision is whether to play Kick
the Can or King of the Hill. A place of
caramel apples and cotton candy, secret
forts, and hopscotch on the streets . . .

Though Celebration appears to be a quintessentially American small town of, say, the 1930s, '40s, or early '50s (I was a little surprised Walt didn't figure out a way to have people live here in black-and-white), it is lacking in certain basic American fundamentals. Take, oh, representative government for example. There isn't one. No mayor. Rather a Disney Company manager. His name is Brent Harrington and he patrols the town in his red Jeep. He has just cracked down on a woman who put up red drapes. Red drapes! What was she *thinking?*

There is a mild underground insurgency growing. I am in Celebration to investigate a rash of law-breaking, of unlawful attempts to introduce some sign of humor and humanity into this Orwellian scene. The situation isn't pretty. Someone or some subversive group is placing plastic pink flamingo lawn decorations in front yards in direct violation of The Declaration, which regulates gnomes, birdbaths, and the like. Plastic pink flamingos are considered perhaps the most egregious violators out there. The cowards usually carry out their dastardly deeds under cover of darkness.

What gives? What's the meaning of this infestation of forbidden flamingos? "I think," says resident Doug Franz, who wrote a book about Celebration, "the pink flamingos are a way of saying, 'This is me. I'm here. I'm not some Disney automaton.' "

So who's responsible for this outbreak of civil disobedience in Disney's residential paradise? Some say Reverend Patrick Wrisley, pastor of the Community Presbyterian Church, might have some answers.

"I don't know who does it," said this mild-mannered preacher, inviting me onto the charming porch of his charming house. (It's always the quiet ones, you know?)

Is there a flamingo underground? "I can't talk about that," Reverend Wrisley replied. We'll see about that. Might change his mind when we get him down to Disney headquarters!

The birds seem to migrate from yard to yard, staying one step ahead of the law. Can plastic flamingos fly? I asked.

"If I told you, I'd have to kill you," he replies. "I . . . I just . . . I can't tell you."

Tough talk from this man of the cloth who does bear an uncanny resemblance to the perpetrator, caught on camera by our tireless night surveillance news team. Whoever's responsible, it only goes to show that the best laid planned communities of mouse and men often go awry.

Reverend Wrisley predicts the flamingos will go forth and multiply. "It's ironic I think," he concludes, "that a plastic, gaudy pink flamingo in the land of the mouse represents reality."

A tip for travelers: most rental car engines cut out at 107 miles per hour. Don't be alarmed; you're not having engine trouble. The rental-car compa-

Pros get the author's bugs off

nies seem to have put some sort of governors on them. Odd that they'd choose one-o-seven.

I know this because I'm always in a hurry and have had opportunities to speed-test them on de-

Mule-train mail in the Grand Canyon

serted stretches of open highways. The first time I hit the one-o-seven barrier was in the Nevada desert a couple of hours north of Las

Dr. Paskowitz at his office

Vegas, headed for Rachel, Nevada, the UFO capital, in a blur of cactus and tumbleweed. The area bears a strong re-semblance to Utah's Bon-

Our big RV in paradise

neville Salt Flats, where Craig Breedlove set all sorts

of land-speed records. He'd go 600 miles per hour! That's 545 miles per hour over the posted speed limit. Think of the points!

My green four-door Pontiac flamed out at one-o-seven in a spot where you could see the road stretching twenty miles ahead from one hilltop to the next. Granted, there were the occasional OPEN RANGE signs, and I had been forced to stop earlier for a herd of cattle being urged across the road by three cowboys on horseback. Had we collided with them at one-o-seven, it would have been steak-human tartare on a warm polenta of pavement.

My next speed test was conducted in northwest Texas, as I was leaving the town of Muleshoe, where I'd spent some time with TV anchorwoman-producer-editor-cameraperson Maggie Reynolds, who worked at a little local station. Very little, very local. She was really the only employee at Channel 6 and the station was in her home, where she broadcast from a spare bedroom — news, weather, and sports — occasionally in her bathrobe. Today's Top Stories: homecoming football ceremonies and an interview with a local boy about his Eagle Scout project.

I was late for a flight out of God-knows-where airport. Muleshoe is near nothing, except Earth, a town eighteen miles away. When

I sped past a sign pointing to Earth, I hit the brakes. Had to see it, maybe take a picture of the sign, purchase a postcard, take home a T-shirt. The side trip to Earth was one I really had no time for so I drove one-o-seven to compensate. I screeched up to a kind of general store, asking the proprietor if she had any Earth ashtrays, T-shirts, or other bric-a-brac. She said she had nothing of the sort, then punched me very hard in the arm and bellowed, "Hey, you're that guy on TV!" I bought a disposable camera and asked the other customer at the store if he'd mind taking my picture at one of the Earth signs coming into town. But while getting into his truck he said that he was sorry, he wasn't "headed that way," even though out of town was about two blocks in every direction. So I just snapped a shot of one of the signs, waved as he drove by in his truck, then sped out of town. At one-o-seven. A couple of weeks later, a newspaper clipping arrived at my office headlined CELEBRITY SPOTTED AT EARTH.

My rented Taurus was held to 102 by 50 mile per hour headwinds in a dust storm south of Beaver, Oklahoma. My most recent *fair* speed run was nocturnal, conducted around midnight in the Nevada desert south of Las Vegas. I was heading for the town of Laughlin, Nevada, where the owner of a big watch-and-clock shop, Ray Lindstrom aka "The Watchman," would oversee a platoon of temporary horologists (no offense) feverishly changing his store's 20,000 timepieces overnight at the advent of daylight saving time.

It was pitch-black. I hadn't seen another car or even a light for miles, and had just said to myself, "They couldn't possibly pay a cop to sit out here in the middle of nowhere to clock cars coming by every half hour," when a uniformed speed-trap operator pulled me over. "Did you know you were going 100 miles per hour?" the officer asked. "Like hell!" I snapped. "I was doing one-o-seven!" Nice fella, the officer. A viewer; *loved* our show; never missed it; gave me the ticket. But he did offer a friendly piece of advice: I could probably get the fine reduced if I showed up in court. So all I had to do was stick around in Searchlight, friggin', Nevada, for three weeks and I'd be golden. Officer, thanks.

Sometimes there are no rental cars. Flying into Cape Girardeau, Missouri, late one night, the rental-car area, such as it was, had closed. There was no such thing as a taxi. The fire chief was there because a private jet had landed and there was some sort of requirement that there had to be fire equipment present whenever this plane landed. He graciously drove me to my motel in his fire truck.

In frigid International Falls, Minnesota, renters are instructed that when they return their cars they are to leave the keys in the ignition with the engine running. In Dallas, you ride a bus to a huge, new, Texas-size rental-car palace with a big bronze cowboy on horseback in the lobby. Yes lobby, with lounge areas and a Starbucks. What are these people doing hanging out in easy chairs, reading their *Wall Street Journal*s and drinking lattes in the car-rental complex? At Hertz in the Liberal, Kansas, airport there are two cars sitting at the front door. We rent them both and when we return them in Amarillo, Texas, not realizing we had a major part of the guy's fleet, he called a bit upset.

We generally return our rental cars looking like the inside of a Dumpster: empty coffee cups, maps, unwanted reference materials, an array of fast-food wrappers, yams when we were doing a yam story, cow chips when we were doing a cow chip story. We also leave behind coffee mugs and T-shirts bearing the name of the town or event we've just visited — given to us as gifts. This sounds insensitive, but my wife banned such items long ago. Occasionally, Avis will thoughtfully FedEx our junk back to us.

Our toughest rental return was in Florida, where we parked beneath a tree in the hotel parking lot and came out the next morning to an astonishing sight. One thousand birds had shat upon our car. Seabirds, said an expert staying in the hotel, who seemed quite fascinated by this carpet bombing that left not more than two or three inches of car showing between any two deposits. Although disgusting, it worked to our advantage. We were there for the Super Bowl, where security was extremely heavy, but every time we approached a security checkpoint, officers waved us through, no questions asked, just to get us out of their sight.

Signs of a Bad Rental Car Company

1. Reasonable rates
2. Long line at So-So Rent-a-Car desk
3. One So-So clerk . . . hooked up to brain wave monitor (which isn't picking up a strong signal)
4. Clerk explains, "Your car is ready, it's just not here yet."
5. Says, "The only other vehicle I have is . . . let me check my computer . . . Ever driven a backhoe?"
6. Their motto: "At So-So We Know Where You Live"
7. Rental form asks for the names of your spouse and children, whether anyone in your family keeps firearms or is trained in

the martial arts, and if you've seen *Goodfellas*

8. Then a rapid series of questions: "Additional coverages? Flood insurance? Fuel option? Our Custom Family Safety Package featuring seat belts and brakes?"

9. Must take bus to off-site rental car depot: Greyhound

10. At depot, agent says, "Your car is in space 2189Z. Do you have anything to eat?"

11. Your car is the little Sport Shittera

12. With 91,000 miles

13. Ashtray full of butts, empty case of beer in backseat, alongside what appears to be a Snapple bottle of urine. Note on dashboard: "At So-So, We Know You Prefer to Clean *Your* Rental Car *Your* Way!"

14. Blood in trunk

15. So-So replaces with more cleanly subcompact Chevrolet Turdelle

16. Body fits in; head does not

17. Exchange for Chrysler Gran Excremente

18. Having declined gas option, you run out before you exit parking lot. Refill.

19. Finally, at exit gate, you forget to ask directions and back up, blowing all four tires

20. Switch to Ford Feceeze

21. Can't tell your white four-door rental car from seventy-five others in motel parking lot
22. Upon returning the car you discover in the fine print that mileage is unlimited "outside North America"
23. You are charged for gas at the "current prevailing price" of $8.88 a gallon
24. The "Free Upgrade" was $31.00 a day
25. Discover that steering wheel, brake, and rearview mirror options were all extra
26. Your total for the two-day rental at $29.95 per day comes to $473.37

WHORES AND WINDEX

PAHRUMP, NEVADA, POP: 24,631

Yes, Nevada is a bleak, alien planet for the most part. But, you have to appreciate a place where anything goes; a place that allowed slot machines and craps tables decades before the rest of the country suddenly embraced this felonious immorality as a good, solid revenue producer, job generator, and budgetary savior.

Nevada was always a welcoming place, where folks didn't mind at all if you set off a nuclear bomb now and then — at a time when most states were outlawing firecrackers.

And it is a state where, to this day, legal prostitution is a local option. Driving through the good-for-nothing, rocky, scrub-brushed landscape on a cross-country tour in our thirty-four-foot RV, we come upon the rural town of Pahrump, Nevada, which greets us with signs for the Rotary Club, the Church of Christ, Kiwanis Club, Moose Lodge, and an upcoming swap meet. And I try to imagine that Norman Rockwell, week-night town meeting, where folks came together after supper to discuss local issues and to see their elected representatives vote in favor of having whores here in their home-town. Brothels generate revenue and job positions — all manner of jobs and in every conceivable position.

Sheri's Ranch here in Pahrump advertises itself as "the closest brothel to Las Vegas, only 55 minutes away!" Vegas, for all of its racy "What Happens Here Stays Here" swagger, has no brothels (although a therapeutic, deep-tissue, sports massage has been known to escalate). Pahrump — "Past and Present Working Towards a New and Better Future" — does.

We pass the Venus Massage Salon, with a sign featuring "Souvenirs!" — somewhat surprising since patrons of such establishments usually try to destroy all evidence of their visits, rather than bringing home mementoes for the kids. Next we see the entrance to the world-famous Chicken Ranch brothel on Homestead Road, then turn into the spacious parking lot (plenty of room for the family RV) of the brand spanking new building that is Sheri's, but could as easily be a new Applebee's had the sign read "Fajitas Con Sizzle," rather than "Girls! Girls! Girls!"

I ring the doorbell and am greeted by a white-haired, mid-sixtyish woman properly dressed for church. Hmmm. Could this be a senior citizen assisted-fornication facility? My (female) producer decides to wait out front in the sunny, 110-degree asphalt parking lot, while the cameraman, soundman, and myself go in on a fact-finding mission.

Inside, the three of us are introduced to a middle-aged woman named Larraine, dressed in business office attire (no cleavage, no thigh, no feathered mules). She gives us a full tour of the facility, including guest rooms, themed guest cottages, and the outdoor swimming pool area. She says that there are plans (since realized) for a spa, as well as for an equestrian center and a PGA golf course — which all seemed very nice, but (like Pilates and knitting classes, for example) hardly necessary to the primary mission of the facility.

Larraine calls the staff together for a lineup that looks a lot like the *Victoria's Secret Fash-*

ion Show on CBS during ratings weeks. She then offers us a drink in the sports lounge. Driving in the desert can give a man a powerful thirst, so we agree. Several staff members accompany us to the lounge, dressed as they are in clothing appropriate to the desert climate — not so much the Lawrence of Arabia look as sheer, cool, and . . . practical.

Larraine shows me a menu, which offers more than the chicken Caesar and the bloomin' onion, I'll tell you. There's the "Straight Lay," which could be fresh eggs; the "Half and Half," which sounds dairy-oriented; and for the lactose intolerant, some continental cuisine, such as "Crème de Menthe French" and "Frappé French."

Perplexed, I head out to the swimming pool, where several of the employees are enjoying a break in their workday grind, sunbathing in floss bikinis and clear plastic high heels. Being well-trained members of the hospitality industry (Hotel-Motel Management grads from UNLV?), they politely ask what they could do for me.

Well, I say, after 5,300 miles of driving, my fantasy is for them to wash the bugs off my windshield. "What do you mean?" asked one called "Dixie." I explain to them that I do not mean this in any figurative sense, but quite literally.

They look at one another quizzically, allow as how this is a little kinky, frankly, but they agree to do it. For $100 an hour. Each.

Three attractive young women wearing string bikinis stand on chairs, lather up my big bus-size windshield, and rub it clean — while I sit behind the wheel and watch. Best I ever had. Not cheap, but a lot of guys would pay $20 a gallon for regular if the Texaco offered this service.

And I do put in for it on my CBS expense report: "$301. Whores and Windex." Accounting kicks back the report, saying they want more information. Perverts.

MOONBURGERS

MOONSHINE, ILLINOIS, POP: 2

Small towns are not generally known for their cuisine, but sometimes the food's pretty good. Order meat loaf, mashed potatoes, barbecue, chicken-fried steak, gravy — all that stuff that leaves you smiling in your casket, although making it harder to close.

Moonshine, Illinois, is home of the widely renowned Moonburger, which some say is the best hamburger in the world.

East central Illinois is a natural spot for great hamburgers. Although embedded in thousands of square miles of corn and soybeans, there's scarcely a vegetarian around, and almost no fish. Growing up in this land-locked area, I wasn't really sure what a fish looked like . . . didn't know they had eyes . . .

thought they were little sticklike things that swam around in a perpetually breaded state until Mrs. Paul caught the buggers and froze 'em. We didn't have fish. Catholics ate Spam on Fridays.

Are the hamburgers at the Moonshine Store "the best in the world"? Well, that's tall talk, but for openers it definitely serves the best burgers in town. In fact, the store *is* the town, the whole town, population: 2. Helen and Roy Lee Tuttle. They live upstairs over their store, the only building, not counting the outhouse across the street, which they call "Sitty Hall." The form of government is Helenic. "What I say goes," Helen explains.

With just two people in town, do Helen and Roy Lee . . . like . . . sell burgers to *each other* or what? No, in fact burger disciples who've heard The Word have made the pilgrimage to this mecca from fifty states, according to the guest book. "And from thirty foreign countries," Helen adds, "Switzerland, Sweden, Japan, Indonesia, Vietnam, Hawaii." (In east central Illinois, Hawaii is considered a foreign country, as it probably should be.)

Finding Moonshine is the biggest challenge in their quest. It's hard to say where it is, really. It's not on the map. It has soundly defeated many a Global Positioning System.

It's officially at the corner of East 300th Road and North 600th Street, south of Interstate 70 someplace, about halfway between Terre Haute, Indiana, and Effingham, Illinois. Some seekers are lucky enough to spot one of the little white wooden arrows with red letters reading MOONSHINE that are tacked to area telephone poles, but most of those have been swiped as souvenirs. It's best to just ask someone, if you can find someone. After traversing the narrow country roads for an hour, I stop a man driving a tractor, who says he can't really explain the directions and kindly leads me there.

The Moonshine Store is an old general store, one of those two-story rectangular cracker boxes with big windows in front and little high windows on the sides, allowing for tall shelves along the inside walls. These used to dot the Midwestern landscape every couple of miles, back when there were lots of family farmers rather than a few agribusiness tycoons like there are now.

Those general stores often featured a post office and sold flour, fabric, overalls, coal oil, farm supplies, and pretty much anything else rural folk needed that they couldn't make themselves. The Moonshine Store is more of a 7-Eleven these days, offering sandwiches, chips, drinks, and random goods such as baseball caps and birdhouses. These old stores were also social centers, and the Moonshine Store still is.

At 5 a.m. the day of my visit, the darkness is illuminated by bright moonlight. Sure enough — the town is named after the pools of moonlight flooding the fields, not the homemade corn liquor some come to Moonshine hoping for.

Delroy, Delmer, and Garyl — three names you won't find in *7,000 Names for Baby* — are already at the store drinking coffee with some of the other regulars. They're wearing plaid shirts, overalls, and baseball caps bearing the names of ag products, and they're talking about the forecast for rain, the corn crop, and deer hunting.

Coffee's a quarter and don't be asking for any lattes. If it's your birthday, you buy coffee for everybody and you bring the doughnuts. "Some come and spend the day sitting in the pews," Helen says, which is not rhetorical but a reference to the only seats in the house: some old church pews, appropriate for eating heavenly burgers.

Some of the men say they've been coming here all their lives, a few on a daily basis. Harold figures he's consumed . . . ohhh . . . about ten thousand burgers here. Everybody laughs, but the figure probably is in the thousands.

Delmar recalls that back in about '51, a few years after the coming of electricity to the area, the store bought the first TV anyone around here had ever seen. "People would come to see *Amos 'n Andy,* or even just the test pattern," he says. That dull around here? "Yep."

Paul remembers people crowding into the store to eat peanuts and drink Cokes while watching the Gillette Friday Night Fights on the TV. "There was an old woman who owned the place sitting in a rocking chair by a potbellied stove," he says. "She had an old hen sitting on a shelf laying eggs." No sell-by date was necessary, but if you needed a dozen you might have to wait.

Helen says the store was built in 1912 after the original burned down. "One woman thought I'd been here since it was built and asked me how I managed to preserve my skin. I told her it was hamburger grease from standing over the grill." Maybe Helen could pick up some extra bucks giving hot animal-fat facial spa treatments.

After peeling onions and slicing tomatoes for the condiment table, she takes a few large rolls of hamburger out of the refrigerator. I sidle up to her, trying to discover the secrets of this world-renowned burgermeister. But all I notice as she cups the burgers with her bare hands (no rubber gloves here) is that the burgers are pretty big. She says they're even bigger when Roy Lee makes 'em. Bigger hands. Bad for profits. The fellow that started White Castle must have had baby hands.

"There's nothing in them," Helen says. "Just straight hamburger. I do buy the best I can get. Each one of them is God blessed, that's what makes 'em so good." No avocado, no Gorgonzola. Just meat and heat. "They must be God blessed," she says, "for people to come here from all over the world."

Helen is as straightforward as her burgers, a good old-fashioned Midwesterner: earnest, hardworking, matter-of-fact. She wears her gray hair sensibly close-cropped, like a marine, for keeping cool over a hot grill as she frys up plain and simple all-American hamburgers. She is uncomfortable discussing her acclaim. "I don't advertise the 'Best Hamburgers,' just 'hamburgers.' " Of course she doesn't advertise them at all.

At 10 a.m., Roy Lee tips back his camouflage cap and lights the small grill — about two-by-two, not much bigger than those installed in upscale, largely unused suburban kitchens these days. Then he goes ahead and puts on the first batch of burgers. So early? Won't they be cold?

Nope. At 10:02 a.m. customers start coming through the front door and ordering: "Two hamburgers," "Eight cheeseburgers and a hamburger," "One burger," "Fourteen cheeseburgers and one double cheeseburger." What meal can this possibly be?

A first-timer orders a grilled chicken sandwich and is politely told to forget it, as are customers ordering "a hot ham-and-cheese" and "a pork tenderloin." Fries, you say? Nope. Chips. One woman says she'll have her hamburger medium rare, but in fact she'll have it medium well because that's how Helen cooks 'em — all of 'em — and "that's how people around here like 'em." Case closed.

Helen does offer other sandwiches (her cold ham-and-cheese is quite popular), but not during the "dinner" — which most of us call "brunch" or "lunch" — rush. During that time, cheeseburgers are as exotic as it gets, although she will make a double cheese and once made a triple! But ordering something other than the burger at this mecca is like going to Morton's Steakhouse and ordering the perch.

Three women assist Helen. They're unpaid

volunteers, except they each get a free burger. One of them, Tracy, has been coming here since she was a baby, according to her father: "We didn't have a baby scale, so we'd bring her here and weigh her on the meat scale." Tracy blushes.

The volunteers bring out the burgers as they come off the grill and set them on a card table, the condiment table, where customers heap 'em high with onions, tomatoes, pickles, mustard, ketchup, and, this being the Midwest, mayonnaise. A customer has brought tomatoes from her garden, so good you could throw away the meat.

By noon the mounted deer head on the wall oversees a packed house. Helen is furiously flipping, and wiping her brow with paper towels. A dog sits by her side, hoping that in her haste she'll accidentally flip one onto the floor again. Customers fill the pews, sit in folding chairs, on a front-porch bench, or at picnic tables in the side yard. Inside, some eat standing up and others sit cross-legged on the floor. Cars and pickup trucks are parked solid out front with the daily overflow across the street in a field.

The store is abuzz. A regular happening, it is, like a potluck supper, a church social, or a cocktail party with burgers not booze. Such sociability, congeniality, community!

Rose, ninety-three years old, says she likes the burgers. A lot. She's been coming here since 1919. Come to think of it there are several regular customers in their nineties, one of whom says she eats a cheeseburger here every day. Could burgers, then, be a key not only to skin care but also to longevity? "Yes, that's possible," Rose says.

"We used to come here on Saturday nights," she says, "by buggy or horseback, but mostly we walked with my dad carrying a lantern. There'd be about a hundred kids playing games in the road outside." Her brother once saved the store from burning down, smothering a fire with twenty-pound bags of flour.

A woman in a long black dress and a white bonnet — said to be a Mennonite — holds her baby with one hand and a Moonburger with the other. In another pew, a very large man in a very wide set of overalls closes his eyes and says grace silently before taking his first bite. He says he eats a burger a day here. He'd like to eat more than one, but his doctor has advised against it. It is suggested he seek a second opinion.

The burgers are $2.25. (Helen has regretfully had to raise the price as meat prices rise.) Payment is by cash only (although Lord only knows where you'd get cash around here) and on the honor system. You put your money in the pile on the counter and take your change. Helen doesn't have time to fool with that. Regulars are billed monthly for their burgers, and for some it must be one of the bigger bills they receive.

At 12:25 p.m., a pickup truck whips into the parking lot, kicking up a cloud of dust. "Did we make it?" the driver shouts. What? "The deadline." They did make it, barely.

At 12:30 p.m. sharp, Helen shuts off the grill and there are no more burgers — no exceptions. How about at, like, 12:31? "They don't get one," she says. And if they plead and beg? "They can come back tomorrow." How about if they came from Japan? "I've heard every excuse," she says, "but it don't get 'em nowhere. We've got rules and regulations." Although she might make them a cold ham-and-cheese to go.

At one o'clock she closes the door and hangs the CLOSED sign on it. "If you're still in here you help clean up," she announces. This day is a good one. She's sold 171 hamburgers and cheeseburgers (the all-time record is 287). Plus chips and drinks. Does she really make any money around here? "I don't," she says. "That's why I'm still around here." Roy Lee drives a bulldozer to make ends meet.

She doesn't know how much longer they can keep it up. "It's hard work, the price of hamburger keeps going up, and we're retirement age," Helen says. "But if nobody takes over I guess we'll have to stay."

People suggest she stay open more hours and put an addition on the building. Has she thought about a drive-thru window? "Nope," she says. "We're gonna keep things the way they always were, the way they are." If anybody can buck the tide of history and keep this old relic hopping, it's Helen.

Is the Moonburger the best hamburger in the world? Well, that's a matter of individual taste. But the Moonshine Store is definitely one of the very best places in the world to eat one.

WATERMELON CAPITAL OF THE WORLD

LULING, TEXAS, POP: 5,080

In Luling, Texas, more citizens vote in the watermelon queen contest than in the mayoral election.

"It's every girl's dream growing up in Luling to be the watermelon queen," says the current reigning monarch, Cathi Johnson, a cute, blondish high-school senior, who is completely surrounded by little girls gazing admiringly upon this chiffoned vision like she's just stepped out of their storybooks.

Driving into Luling, you sense the importance of watermelon right away, from the moment you spot the water tower, painted dark green with light green stripes to look just like a big juicy one.

It's one of half a dozen towns in America

306

calling itself the "Watermelon Capital," but Luling backs it up, with the water tower and a four-day annual festival called the Luling Watermelon Thump — thump, of course, being what you do to a melon to see if it's ripe. Events include the Thump Queen coronation, the big Thump Parade, a biggest-melon contest and auction, and a watermelon-seed "spit-off" that's held in a permanent seed-spitting arena called the Luling Spitway. No other so-called "Watermelon Capital" comes close. Hard to believe now, but when the town decided to have a festival back in 1954, they almost went with tomatoes!

This community, south of Austin and east of San Antonio, used to be a big oil town, growing from five hundred to five thousand residents when there was a big strike back in the 1920s. All the oilfield roughnecks, most of whom lived here in tents, earned Luling the mantle of "toughest little town in Texas," but these days the only remnants of that era are a few pump jacks — and they're painted up with watermelons.

A group of men, farmers most of them, stand outside the old feed store downtown, scrutinizing and discussing the impressive watermelons on display in the front window.

"Good year," says one. "Yup," concurs another. "It was," offers a third.

Bubba Damon, a thirtysomething melon farmer who wears a Fu Manchu mustache, jeans, denim shirt, boots, and a cowboy hat, has what he believes could be the biggest melon in town this year. And he ain't just braggin'.

An authorized, certified, deputized watermelon contest official comes out to Bubba's melon patch to cut a few off his vines for entry in the competition. Got to make sure the biggest watermelon in Luling (a singular achievement) is *from* Luling. Don't want somebody sneaking in a melon from Soda Springs or Saturn.

Bubba's biggest watermelon sits in a wire cage with a protective tarp over it to ward off any number of varmints, like rabbits, deer, and coyotes, which might want to eat it (not realizing it was a competition melon). Bubba says he's gone all-out this year: moving his crop of black diamond melons to a new field of sandy loam atop clay — perfect soil for sprouting great big watermelons. He's plowed around the young plants with an antique cultivator, and powders the melons with talc to avoid sunburn rot. Around here they pamper their melons like thoroughbred racehorses.

Once this biggest melon is cut from the vine by the contest official, Bubba picks it up to examine the bottom for signs of rot. He's relieved to find none. No one likes to admit it, but in today's society, a watermelon's looks count some too. He carries it to the pickup truck for the ride into town and a place of honor alongside nineteen others in the store window.

Next day, there's the big weigh-in to determine the title. A postal employee brings over a scale and weighs the entries. The newly crowned Thump Queen, wearing her sash and crown, sits regally at a small table recording the results as part of her official duties. She shows no emotion lest it be taken as favoritism. There are melons weighing in the thirty-, forty-, and fifty-pound ranges. Then comes Bubba's big melon and the postman calls out, "Sixty-one pounds, five ounces." And don't think that doesn't set the crowd buzzing.

Then another thirtyish farmer with a Fu Manchu, Robert Watts, walks up with a whopper, and the crowd is stilled. The postman squints and nudges the little weight on the scale another hair before announcing, "Sixty-two pounds, six ounces." And the crowd gasps; some of 'em, anyway. Robert, wearing a Watts Waterwell Service cap is this year's grand champion. He's from a long line of big melon growers. His grandfather, Pappy, holds the all-time record: eighty pounds, eight ounces. Think of it! Bubba, the reserve champion, says in an exclusive postgame interview that he's vowing to strive even harder next year.

Then the top melons are whisked away to the main pavilion for the big auction. In Luling, it's prestigious to own a big watermelon, and a couple hundred people are sitting in the audience — sitting on their hands, many of them, so as not to be mistaken for bidders — as onstage the auctioneer goes to town.

"Heygimmetwonowthreenowfourhundredhup!FiveletmeseesixIgotseveneightoverheregentlemaninthegreenshirtnowathousandhup!Nowgivemeelevenhundred! . . ."

Bubba's big melon goes for $4,300! More than even the biggest melon for some reason. Not bad, considering the growers only get about ten cents a pound for their melons when they sell them as produce. But these are celebrity melons and that's the way it goes in today's world, where — fair market value — Paris Hilton would be worth about ten cents a pound too.

Half the town turns out for the annual coronation of a new Thump Queen, who's elected by popular vote after an intense, two-month campaign that involves wallpapering the town with posters and sending out squads of workers to canvass door-to-door.

When reigning Thump Queen Catherine Johnson is announced, she walks as a queen does, slowly and gracefully up the center aisle on a carpet red-as-a-ripe-one. Three attendants hold her long train, heavily laden with embroidered and bejeweled watermelons, until she takes her rightful place on the throne.

The outgoing Queen Catherine thanks dozens of people, but much of her farewell address is devoted to Bubba Damon. Much. On twenty-five Saturday mornings during the past year, Bubba has hitched up the elaborate Luling watermelon parade float to his truck, towed it over to Catherine's house, picked her up, and headed out on the highway to another parade in another central or east Texas town. What a sight that must be! Bubba driving down the highway towing a parade float.

Now, you might think the Luling Watermelon Parade wouldn't be much to see. Well, it looks like the friggin' Rose Bowl Parade! There are bagpipers, mariachi bands, cloggers, polka dancers, and queens upon queens, maybe twenty different queens from twenty different towns: a bluebonnet queen, peach queen, even a watermelon queen from another town!

In her farewell address, Queen Catherine speaks with emotion, "Bubba truly made an impact on me . . . Bubba taught me to just lay back and laugh . . . One time I passed out and Bubba threw me over his shoulder . . . The Saturdays that were the best were just me and Bubba, the two of us . . . Thanks, Bubba, for making this year everything I wanted and some things I didn't want."

About half of the former Thump Queens attend the coronation, including the first one crowned half a century ago, Bettie Sue Blackwell Towns. She says that like most everything these days, there is less formality now. "We had brunches and teas and the queen's dance at the country club with an orchestra." But she says it's still a very big deal in Luling. "You talk to any of these little girls and they'll all say 'I'm gonna be Thump Queen when I get big.' "

The four smiling contestants vying to wear Queen Catherine's crown for the next year walk, somewhat less gracefully than she, up the red carpet holding bouquets of roses and curtseying before Her Highness. They are Brandy, Catherine, Rebecca, and finally Jessica, a stunning Hispanic girl — tall, dark, and beautiful — who looks more like a contestant for Miss World than Thump Queen.

After much ado, the new Thump Queen is announced. It is not, to my amazement, Miss World, but rather the ample, normal-enough-looking daughter of a prominent local merchant. And so it goes.

Christie Rheinboldt could teach the Pentagon something about "shock and awe." She's the *twelve*-time watermelon speed-eating champion of Luling, Texas — and therefore the world. She has trophies and medals and a copy of her photo in *Sports Illustrated*!

The husky twenty-one-year-old redhead can obliterate and devour a big quarter-melon slice in as little as twenty-four seconds, leaving other contestants, frankly, shocked and awed. "I don't play around," the champ says.

Her mother remains . . . awed. "She devours watermelon very quickly — very, very quickly. At last year's contest when Christie sat down at the table, half the other contestants got up and walked off." Not even Muhammad Ali's opponents did that, even in his prime.

It isn't pretty. When the starter yells "Go," Christie buries her face in the watermelon, using what she calls a "typewriter" style, which doesn't begin to describe her speed and ferocity. Think pull-start, chain-saw typewriter. She viciously sweeps her head back and forth, back and forth, ripping through the melon with her teeth as the red flesh flies. "You don't take a breath, you lose if you take a breath," she explains. "I don't chew, I swallow." When she hits the white rind, her head bobs up and she begins stuffing the far-flung remnants of the devastating attack into her mouth with both hands. Talk about conspicuous consumption. The only thing faster would be dynamite.

"We're so proud of her," beams her mother, who is her biggest and most vocal fan. "I yell and scream worse than Little League parents."

If the rules required her to eat the rind and the table, Christie would. To gain a full appreciation, I don swimming goggles and a huge trash bag, and take her on at a picnic table in her backyard. It was "ready, set, go" and — Bang! she was finished and laughing at me.

Next day she arrives at the pavilion for the championship with her family, all wearing T-shirts proclaiming, variously, "I Am the Proud Mother/Father/Brother of the Watermelon Eating Champion." Hers reads, "I AM the Watermelon Eating Champion."

There are preliminary contests for youngsters, which are charming. The winner of the beginners division is a boy who looks to be about six years old and who may have suffered hearing loss from his mother yelling "Eat, Michael, Eat!" at the top of her lungs directly into his ear. When the eating's over his stuffed cheeks are puffed out, and he has a look on his face that would definitely make you stop the car if the family was on a trip.

This seems to be the way the watermelon speed-eating contest was intended: a fun event with kids and parents getting messy and laughing a lot. But you know Americans: pretty soon we're applying for Olympic status and wearing Nike watermelon-eating shoes.

The main event is serious business. About fifty adults, mostly men, sit down on both sides of a long, long picnic table and quarter-melon slices are placed before each of them. Christie remarks disdainfully and to no one in particular, "I can eat this in twenty-four seconds," perhaps trying to psych out a few of her competitors. And judging by the looks on their faces, it's working. "I don't play around," she says, glowering like Mike Tyson used to before knocking out an opponent in the first round. She is ravenous, having starved herself all day.

The problem is that the judging in this sport has not come up to the level of the intense competition. How many judges are needed? What are the criteria for winning? When all the red and pink are gone? What?

Christie puts her mouth down on the end of the slice (the left margin of the typewriter), the chief judge yells "Go," and Christie obliterates her prey. One of the judges nearby says she's won, so she stops. But the chief judge does not see or hear this and the others keep eating away until a man from out of town is proclaimed the winner. Christie's appeals fall on deaf ears. She flings her melon rind at her mother, then gets up from the table and stalks off. She is awarded third place. She scowls in the group picture of the winners and vows never to return.

Much as our president throws out the first pitch of the baseball season, Her Royal Highness Queen Rebecca spits out the first seed at the world championship of watermelon-seed spitting. *Tastefully*, of course, keeping one hand on her crown so it doesn't come flying off when she thrusts her head forward during the classic spitting delivery.

Before the games begin, the crowd is encouraged to sing a kind of seed-spitting anthem: "Gonna blow that seed with all my might . . . gonna send that seed on a record flight . . ." And so on. Sadly, few know the words.

It's a standing-room-only crowd, five deep in places, here at the Spitway, a facility described by Jamie Nickells — yes, of the famed spittin' Nickells family — as "the finest spitting venue in the world today." And you know what? It *is*.

So many wish to spit competitively that officials have instituted a lottery system to limit entries to forty in the Adult Open division. Spitters have come from throughout the known spitting world, from Dripping Springs and Houston, California (the state) and Switzerland (the country). A contestant from Hopeville, Illinois, says he's been practicing by spitting corn. "Completely different," a Texas spitter remarks, and indeed the corn-spitter doesn't spit the watermelon seed very far at all. More like he drooled it.

Sweet little girls in watermelon dresses spit, as do big men in watermelon shirts, baseball caps, cowboy hats, and watermelon boots. Some do warm-up exercises with their face, and neck muscles, others stay loose with beer. Some hold their beer cans while they spit. Try that at Wimbledon or Augusta National.

One advocate of beer as a performance enhancer is Aaron Nickells, son of Jamie and the defending world champion. (Hey, Babe Ruth wasn't exactly drinking Gatorade you know.) The eighteen-year-old employs the popular "cannon style," wherein the spitter curls the tongue into a barrel around the seed, takes a deep breath, and fires down range.

Jamie's brother, Walter, former world champion, emphasizes the importance of trajectory. "Spit 'em at forty-five degrees," he advises, "and they'll roll better once they hit." Yes, the spitter gets the roll. Seed selection is also critical: big, black, heavy seeds are the best for distance spitting.

All the best spitters seem to come from Luling, a place where everyone says spitting watermelon seeds is a part of summertime. Walter laments the advent of the seedless watermelon, saying, "They make me sick."

"As kids, we'd always spit seeds at each other for entertainment," recalls the legendary Lee Wheelis, a long, tall Texan, who one historic day back in 1989 spit a watermelon seed sixty-eight feet, nine and one-eighth inches! Seriously. It was, of course, a new world record and still stands today. Needless to say, his life changed. "People started calling me for radio interviews," he says, "and kids at church asked me for my autograph. It was overwhelming.

"It's a gift," Lee explains. "You either got it or you don't." He says that chewing tobacco keeps him in top spitting form.

But this is not to be the day for Lee, or for Aaron. Most of the entrants in the champions' division are spitting in the forty-foot range.

But when Jamie Nickells, the spit-off announcer, urges former champ and Lulingian Kay Edwards to "Be the seed!" she uncorks a whale of an expectoration: fifty feet! No separate women's division necessary in this sport.

Another Luling product, Richard Robbins, a big man, steps into the box and lets fly a mighty spit. He does fifty-two feet, seven inches to take the first-place trophy. It has a golden figure on top, which is a . . . what is it? It's a swimmer . . . or perhaps a diver with his knees slightly bent. They don't have spitting trophies or Dritex spitting jerseys or Pro-Spit shoes. Yet.

THE NATION'S ICEBOX

INTERNATIONAL FALLS, MINNESOTA, POP: 6,332

International Falls, Minnesota, claims the title "Coldest Spot in the Nation," and you'd think they'd be welcome to it. Nope. Proud residents of Embarrass, Minnesota (all 691 of them), are fighting for the honor. While folks over in Tower, Minnesota (population: 479), claim it's colder there than either of them.

Notice that not too many people live in any of these towns. Who'd want to? Why did all the Scandinavian immigrants fight their way 1,500 miles across the country seeking a colder way of life? Why didn't they head straight down to Miami Beach? Or Boca?

My first story in Minnesota — or Minnesooota, the preferred pronunciation —

was in Eveleth, where it was twenty below zero, and the favorite winter pastime seemed to be drinking peppermint schnapps and curling, that peculiar-looking game of shuffleboard on ice that employs a strong element of housekeeping. Curling clubs up here north of Duluth are social centers (perhaps because they're a balmy twenty-eight degrees inside), and nothing beats a bonspiel (curling tournament), where locals compete for toasters and jackknives. There was a big one going on in Eveleth, with sixteen teams, including the U.S. Olympic Curling Team, which actually lost to a local team, but did manage to out-drink them during the match. A few hours after explaining to me that curlers are well-conditioned athletes, a beer-bellied Olympian was running up and down our motel hallway completely blitzed, yelling and wearing a woman's mink coat.

I learned a little about curling, and about Minnesota winters; how people adapt to the inhuman cold by learning to never go outside; how some buy big furry dogs to sleep with and plug in their cars to keep them warm overnight. I walked out of the motel to unplug my car, and when I bent down, both lenses fell out of my glasses.

On my next visit, I flew into Minneapolis one evening when it was ten below. That was the temperature, not the windchill factor. Minnesotans think the windchill factor is for wimps. I fought my way from the hotel to a restaurant a block away, my mustache freezing, my head aching from the cold, my nose running, fingers numbing, ears burning — and arrived feeling as though I'd walked the Iditarod on all fours. A waitress waltzed over and greeted me with: "Still nice out there?"

I guess she meant not a blizzard. Frankly, I thought the state should be applying for disaster relief funds, but everyone says that here you just bundle up, go out, and enjoy winter. These are blood ancestors of those immigrants who struggled and died in their relentless search for the most miserably cold part of the country.

Perfect for ice fishing, which is shivering while staring at a hole in the ice. To me, ice fishing is the gold standard of how far men will go to avoid their spouses.

Every winter on Lake Mille Lacs an entire town of some five thousand ice-fishing houses springs up, complete with street signs. You see this whole town of "Frostbite Flats" out there sitting on the frozen water. You see lots of cars and trucks. Yet there is a cracking sound as you drive onto the lake, a sound that's caused passengers to leap from their cars. Trying to make me even more uncomfortable, a fisherman out there tells me that a guy once felt a tug on his line, reeled it in, and found a license plate on the end. His. He ran outside and his truck had fallen through the ice. Although probably untrue, it's a good story.

The ice town started long ago with a few shacks (perhaps shanties, but that's not important right now). This day the ice houses range from a blue tarpaulin draped over a lone sitting fisherman, to houses the size of manufactured homes (and some are), eight by twelve to twelve by forty-six, even two-story models, equipped with TVs, thermostats, carpeting, bathrooms, cookstoves, and refrigerators to keep the beer warm (thirty-three plus degrees). There are ice-house rental agencies.

Many ice anglers have hooked up elaborate alarm systems to alert them when a fish is on the line: flip-up flags, buzzers, bells, whistles, even car alarms. It's tough enough trying to drink cheap brandy, watch a football game, and play poker without having to pay attention to your fishing line.

Then came my visit to International Falls, "The Nation's Icebox," on the Canadian border, a town where manufacturers test new products to see how they react to extreme cold. It had been a very cold winter across the nation, but it apparently wasn't frigid enough for some of the perverse, who were coming in droves to be in the most miserably cold spot in the nation. They didn't know about Tower, which holds the record for the all-time record low in Minnesota at sixty below, or Embarrass, which has hit fifty-seven below but argues vehemently that day in, day out it's more wretchedly cold than either of the others. Despite the arguments, International Falls enjoys the big reputation. Russia used to punish political dissidents by banishing them to places like this, but in America? It's a tourist destination.

In International Falls, business is booming, with nary a motel room to be had. Why? "No bugs," answers one visitor. "We just had to see the coldest spot," says another. "The first day we were here it was minus forty!" exudes yet another, gleefully. "I've never been this cold in my life!" She's visiting from Texas where it was one hundred degrees warmer when she left home. There's a tour bus pulling in filled with folks on a four-day cold-weather excursion.

The next morning, it is forty-five below. They say it's not that bad, if you dress for it. They're full of it. PETA would not like it here. People are layered in fox, beaver, mink, coyote, elk, lambs wool, and goat hair that cover their heads, ears, hands, feet, legs, and torsos. Everyone wears a ski mask. (I guess when you rob a 7-Eleven here you take it off.) We see a group of snowmobilers who have duct-taped their entire faces with slits for the eyes and nose, but even that isn't enough. They have to give up.

So what do people do when they get here? Some seem to spend most of their time calling home and telling everyone how cold it is, and that if you, like, leave a banana in your car overnight you can drive nails with it. That's what they say.

If it would warm up a little, say to maybe minus ten or so, they could engage in local sports like schmooshing, which involves four people attaching each of their left feet to one two-by-four board and each of their right feet to another, then racing another four-schmoosher team in a shopping center parking lot. This is a non-Olympic winter sport, apparently the result of extreme cabin fever and attempts to treat the fever with nonprescription brandy and schnapps. This may offer us a window into how a pro wrestler was elected governor.

We drive our rental car back to the little airport, heeding the sign DO NOT TURN OFF YOUR RENTAL CAR. LEAVE YOUR RENTAL CAR AT THE FRONT DOOR WITH

THE ENGINE RUNNING. Starting a car in this climate can be an all-day job.

Our small plane takes off on a completely snow-packed runway, assuming there is a runway somewhere under all that.

And looking down at the frozen Northland, it occurs to me that maybe a trip to International Falls could make sense in a certain way. You know how you hate to come home from a winter trip to Maui or the Caribbean? From here, it's an absolute pleasure.

The Holy Grail of Roadside Attractions

CAWKER CITY, KANSAS, POP: 521 (ET AL.)

The World's Largest Ball of Twine is the holy grail of roadside attractions. Three balls currently claim the title.

There is a roiling — OK, simmering — debate about who has the world's biggest twine ball. "Why?" is not an acceptable question. A good deal of civic pride is involved and no one wants to tout theirs as the "World's Second Largest Ball of Twine" — although that does have a ring to it.

Cawker City, Kansas, claims to have the World's Largest Ball of Twine displayed in a place of honor, right downtown, under its new gazebo. Local resident Frank Stoeber wound 1,600,000 feet of twine into a ball 11 feet in diameter — only a foot shy of the

Darwin, Minnesota, champion when he passed away.

But townspeople have continued Frank's work, and their ball is now thought to be bigger than the one in Minnesota. The town holds an annual Twine-A-Thon and sells souvenirs. I highly recommend the Cawker City twine ball salt-and-pepper set, among the best in my collection.

The day we stopped at the twine ball, three farmers who'd driven down from Nebraska to see it were admiring the fibroid sphere. They seemed most impressed, commenting: "Wow!" "Man, that's big!" "THAT is one big ball of twine!" What *does* one say in the presence of such an immense ball of twine?

Darwin, Minnesota (pop: 276), claims the title for what it says is a 17,400-pound ball, 12 feet in diameter, created by one man Francis A. Johnson, who is said to have wound string four hours a day for thirty-nine years. Instead of hospitalizing and medicating the man for obsessive-compulsive disorder, Francis was hailed for his dedication. He only gave up his winding when they pried the twine from his cold, dead hands.

He wound the ball on his farm, then moved it to a circular shed — open in front so all could see — in his front yard, something that would get you a stiff fine in any respectable suburb. Instead, the town built a new shelter for it and started a Twine Ball Days.

And lest you, for some stupid reason, have any doubt about the drawing power of twine, the third claimant on the World's Largest Ball of Twine title is the centerpiece of the Ripley's Believe It or Not in Branson, Missouri. It was purchased at a price of $20,000 to $30,000 from its creator, J. C. Payne of Valley View, Texas (pop: 737). Notice how really large twine balls all come from really small towns? You never see people on city sidewalks rolling twine.

We visited J.C. at his ranch on the day the big ball was shipped to Branson. He said he started collecting twine from hay bales. Then he and his wife, Elsie Ruth, began driving around north Texas asking cattlemen and dairy farmers for their twine. Hearing of his quest to create the world's largest ball, people from all over were moved to bring and mail him twine. It was accepted into the Guinness World Records, where it replaced the Darwin ball, apparently based on its diameter and circumference. Some in the twine-balling community say it's just because J.C.'s ball is made of colorful plastic twines, which makes it prettier for the tourists in Branson. I hope they're wrong about that.

Calling to mind the multitudes that lined the railroad tracks carrying President Lincoln's body from Washington, D.C., to Springfield, Illinois, or perhaps those who lined the 405 Freeway to witness O.J.'s chase, crowds showed up at predetermined truck stops in Oklahoma to see the twine ball as it made its way from Texas to Ripley's, where it was expected to be a bigger draw than either the two-headed calf or the aircraft carrier made of matchsticks.

And, although a sign next to Cawker City's ball reads THRIFT + PATIENCE = SUCCESS, I doubt that Frank Stoeber had any such lesson in mind. It's nice to see, in these days of self-important people doing "relevant" things ("Fishing Not Drugs," "Pizza for Peace"), that some are still doing things simply for the hell of it.

THE NAPA VALLEY
OF COW CHIPS

BEAVER, OKLAHOMA, POP: 1,478

At the Iowa State Fair I happen to notice that the cow chips being used in the cow chip throwing contest are imported!

Why in the world would a state like Iowa — with 3.8 million cows, more cows than people! — *import* cow chips? That's my question.

"Because ours are the finest cow chips in the world today," explains cow-chip aficionado Kirk Fisher, standing in a field of chips outside Beaver, Oklahoma, a small town in the panhandle. "This is the cow chip capital."

And proud of it! "I'm so proud that we have the world, not just the state or national, but the world cow chip capital right here in my district," proclaims State Representative Gus Blackwell, in town for the World Championship Cow Chip Throwing Contest. He says originally there were some in the state capital who were not on board with the whole cow dung thing: "Our state tourism department threw away almost $60,000 worth of brochures that featured the cow chip because they did not want that image projected."

Beaver is a cow town (and by the way, we don't need any more snickering in the back about beavers, or jokes about the liquor store changing its name to Beaver Liquors). Just outside the city limits, cowboys herd cows in cow pastures full of cow chips. The "fruited plain" indeed. I watch as calves are roped, branded with a hot poker, then castrated by a woman with a knife. How's *your* day going?

A cute little figure named King Cow Chip is the town's registered trademark. A fifteen-foot plastic beaver stands in the middle of town . . . eating a cookie? No, holding a cow chip. The statue is mobile and rolls down the street in the annual Cow Chip Parade that precedes the World Championship Cow Chip Throw.

"We live out here in the middle of nowhere," says a woman watching the parade and speaking the truth. "We need to be known for something. If this is what it's for, then I guess we'll take it."

Locals believe the Beaver chip to be the Rolls-Royce of cow chips, or meadow muffins, whichever you prefer. "Our short prairie grass and clear water just produce a better chip," says Kirk, a founder of the chip toss thirty-seven years ago. "Then the chips sit out here on these prairies in the Oklahoma winds and season just right so they're ready for tossing in the spring."

With such perfect conditions, Beaver is a veritable Napa Valley of cattle dung, so good it's exported not only to Iowa but throughout the nation and the world. In these brand-conscious times, the beaver on the box is your assurance of the finest in cow chips.

You may be surprised to learn that cow chips played an excrementally vital role in the settlement of the Great Plains.

"Cow chips were actually a very important part of our culture out here," Kirk explains. "We don't have many trees and so the only thing our ancestors had to heat their homes and cook their food was cow chips." They burn. Today energy experts are looking at the two hundred million tons of pasture patties produced by these fine bovine Americans as an affordable, renewable source of electric power. Kirk says the tossing of the chips is also part of their pioneer heritage. "As they were gathering chips they'd see who could throw it farthest and get it in the wagon."

Before the World Championship comes the spring harvest by the Appropriations Committee. Kirk walks among the chips, like Goldilocks, looking for piles that are not too big and not too small, not too fresh and not too old and disintegrated. The cow pie needs to have structural integrity for proper flight.

He fearlessly picks up one with his bare hands. No gloves? No tongs? "No," he says, "they're thrown with bare hands. Good throwers lick their fingers between their first and second throws. Nothing to fear, this has no odor at all."

Contestants come from far and wide. Defecation is ubiquitous. "They've shown up from Australia. Japan seems to have a fascination with chip tossing. Germany. A young lady from South Africa. So it's an international event," Kirk says. Even so, local fireman James Pratt and his daughter Terri are the reigning men's and women's world champions. James has been on the chip-tossing circuit and he, too, thinks Beaver's are best. "I threw in Nebraska and theirs didn't seem as stable as ours. I'm not knocking Nebraska." No, you really don't want to knock another state's fecal matter.

Local champions from other towns are invited here to sling the old dung discus at the World Championship. "Can you just imagine," says Kirk, "the pride in an individual, you know in Iowa or somewhere that wins a sanctioned (sanctioned!) throw and wins an expense-paid trip to Beaver, Oklahoma, to the World Championship Cow Chip Throw?"

No, I can't.

Well, that dream come true is *exactly* what happened to Jessica and Eric when they won in Tilden, Nebraska. They were awarded $200 for their trip to Beaver. That may not sound like much, but the Beaver Motel is $37.50 a night (which was a little high, frankly), and dinner at a local restaurant ten bucks.

"It was a really good prize," Eric enthuses, with Jessica commenting: "We didn't have anything else to do this weekend."

Another top chip chucker, Terri, is a perennial champion in Sauk Prairie, Wisconsin, a state with major cow dung. "God gifted me with a great left arm," she explains, and she believes she's making the most of that gift.

And why did Dina, a rookie, come all the

way from Wyoming? "To throw some crap around," she answers. "I'm always looking for new ways to challenge myself athletically, and being able to be on the field at a world championship is an opportunity I couldn't pass up."

In the championship competition, there's a separate category for politicians. "Because we sling so much, so often," explains Gus, "it's unfair for us to compete with other people."

They sling these meadow muffins in a variety of styles: sidearm, underhand, and barefoot. James, the defending champion, unleashes a mighty heave of two hundred feet (!), which would have been a new world record but for those disqualifying trailing winds (fifty miles per hour this day) that famously come sweeping down the plain here in Oklahoma.

And when all the dung is flung, Dana, a six-time champion from Beaver, wins the women's title again, and has this closing thought: "Oddly enough throwing poop has put me on TV. That's weird. I don't know if that's weird for me to throw poop or for the TV people to find it interesting. But it's weird."

ACKNOWLEDGMENTS

In print, reporters do almost all of the work and receive almost all of the credit; in TV, reporters/correspondents get almost all the credit despite producers, editors, and camera crews doing most of the work. I want to thank the scores of my CBS colleagues who've made my continuing transition from ink-stained wretch to TV guy easier, while I've indubitably made things harder for them.

Thanks to resourceful producers, artistic editors, and camera crews — who I find extraordinary creatures of the modern age, requiring the patience of Job, an artist's eye, sharp ears, strong back, good mind, technical know-how, a degree of daring (or foolhardiness), the gifts of clairvoyance and omniscience, an imperviousness to foul weather, and the ability to go for prolonged periods without food, water, or rest, as well as the willingness to shoot from the hood of my moving car, or in total darkness, underwater, in pigpens, in minus-forty-degree temperatures, or riding backwards on a horse, no hands, shouldering a thirty-pound camera down a sheer wall of the Grand Canyon. Oh, and they must suffer fools gladly. Thanks for that. When the crews laugh, I know it's right. When they say something clever, I steal it immediately.

PHOTO CREDITS

ABOUT THE AUTHOR

Bill Geist is an Emmy Award–winning correspondent and commentator for CBS News, appearing weekly on *CBS Sunday Morning* and contributing to the *CBS Evening News* and *48 Hours,* as well as to CBS Sports coverage of the Olympic Games, the Super Bowl, the World Series, and the Final Four. He is the bestselling author of six previous books: *Little League Confidential; The Big Five-Oh! — Fearing, Facing, and Fighting 50; City Slickers; Fore! Play* (it's about golf); *Monster Trucks and Hair-in-a-Can — Who Says America Doesn't Make Anything Anymore?*; and *The Zucchini Plague and Other Tales of Suburbia.* Geist and his wife, Jody, have two children, Willie and Libby, and live in New York City.